RUN *the* RACE!

DISCOVER YOUR PURPOSE and EXPERIENCE the POWER of BEING on GOD'S WINNING TEAM

CHRISTINE CAINE

ZONDERVAN®

ZONDERVAN

Run the Race!
Copyright © 2014, 2018 by Christine Caine
Derived from material previously published in *Unstoppable*.
Abridgment by Meredith Hinds.

Requests for information should be addressed to:
Zondervan, *3900 Sparks Dr. SE, Grand Rapids, Michigan 49546*

ISBN 978-0-785-23064-9 (softcover)
ISBN 978-0-310-10819-1 (ebook)

Published in association with the literary agency of David O. Middlebrook, 4501 Merlot Avenue, Grapevine, Texas 76051.

Cover design: Jamie DeBruyn
Interior design: Emily Ghattas

Printed in the United States of America

19 20 21 22 23 24 25 26 27 28 / LSC / 10 9 8 7 6 5 4 3 2

CONTENTS

ONE

THE DIVINE RELAY

can't believe we're here at the Olympics! The Olympics, Nick! Isn't it awesome?"

He could barely hear me above the roar of the crowd.

"Awesome!" he shouted back.

We took in the view together—the massive stadium filled with light and color and motion and 110,000 spectators, the buzz of conversations in who knew how many languages, the red track below, and the runners taking their positions.

The year was 2000—Saturday, September 30. The place, Sydney, in my homeland. I'd celebrated my thirty-fourth birthday a week before, and being here felt like the best birthday gift of my life.

Though I'm Australian by birth, Greek blood runs through my veins. The image of the five interlocking Olympic rings fluttering on the Olympic flags above us and plastered all over Sydney made my heart swell.

I love all things sport and always have. I competed as a runner in high school, and running is still my favorite workout. As a spectator, I've always been partial to the 4 x 100-meter relay, and the women's relay in particular. My husband, Nick, and I were about to watch this very race in person. Eight countries were competing in the final race for gold. I was cheering for the USA team to take the medal.

Before the 2000 Sydney Olympics, the USA women's 4 x 100-meter relay team had won the gold medal nine times out of sixteen Olympics. They were the reigning Olympic champions.

Nick and I watched the runners moving onto the track, four per team. White lines marked the three exchange zones, each 20 meters in length, in every lane. The first runner, the starter, would cover about 100 meters and enter the first exchange zone to meet the second runner, who would already be running, arm stretched out behind, hand open, ready to receive the baton that had to be handed off within that 20-meter exchange zone. Runner two would carry the baton to the second exchange zone and hand off the baton to runner three, who in turn would run about 100 meters, handing off the baton to the anchor, who would carry it across the finish. The entire race would be only one lap, 400 meters, and take less than one minute.

The runners took their positions. A hush fell over the crowd.

The shot rang out and they were off. The first USA handoff was smooth, and my cheers were lost in the roar around me as the US team took the lead. But in the next exchange zone, the second runner struggled to get the baton into the third runner's hand. My heart fell. That muffed handoff had cost precious milliseconds and perhaps the race.

The seconds flew by—41.95 seconds to be exact. That's how long it took for Bahama to win the gold. Jamaica was a mere .18 seconds behind, followed by the USA, at 42.20 seconds, trailing the winning team by .25 seconds.[1]

"Nick, they should have won!" I cried in disbelief. "How did this happen?" He didn't need to answer. It had happened in the fraction of a second in the second handoff. I watched the screen replay the final seconds at the finish line. Exhilaration on the face of the Bahamian anchor, disbelief on the face of the American. I thought my heart would break for her and her team.

"At least they medaled," Nick said. "They won the bronze."

Those women hadn't come for the bronze. They'd come for the gold. They were running to *win*.

Four years passed.

In a hotel room in the US, on August 27, Nick

and I sat in front of a television, captivated by scenes of the 2004 Summer Olympics in Athens, Greece. My eyes were glued to the screen every available moment, but never was my anticipation higher than when Team USA took their places for the first round of the qualifying heats of the women's 4 x 100 relay.

The American women were considered the four fastest runners on the field. Poor Nick was nearly deaf from my screams of joy when they proved themselves to be the fastest and strongest team in the first heat that day: 41.67 seconds!

The next day, nothing could have kept me away from watching the finals, the medal race. When Marion Jones, the second runner, received her baton and accelerated, I knew nothing would stop this incredible team. She approached Lauryn Williams for the second exchange of the baton.

"No!" I screamed, jumping to my feet. "No way!"

Had Lauryn started too early, too fast? Was Marion too far behind? No matter which of them was at fault, when that baton finally passed from Marion's forward thrusting arm to Lauryn's back-stretched hand, they had run *out* of the exchange zone.

But they were the fastest! They were the strongest! They had the lead! They were the best!

It didn't matter. Not only did they miss the gold, they were disqualified. Stopped in their tracks. Not even a *bronze* medal. Once again, they were undone in the exchange zone.

"How could this happen?" I cried.

Nick was a wise enough husband not to offer a response.

Fast-forward to Beijing in 2008, the semifinals—Thursday, August 21. This year, Nick and I, again traveling in ministry, watched from a cottage in the town of Ulverston, Cumbria, England. Exchange one—perfect! Exchange two—ideal! Whew! I was on my feet, screaming. Leading the race, Torri Edwards reached forward for that final exchange to Lauryn Williams ...

What happened next is still seared in my memory—the image of that baton slipping from Lauryn Williams's grasp and hitting the track. She dropped the baton! Dropped it! And with it the hopes and dreams of every fan of Team USA. Disqualified in the semifinals! For the first time since 1948,[2] Team USA wouldn't even run in the final medal race. I was speechless, which, if you ask Nick, was a miracle in itself.

THE GAMES GO ON AND ON AND ON ...

By the time of the London 2012 games, I was afraid to watch the women's 4 x 100 relay.

Not that I was going to let that stop me, of course. I assumed it was my love of the games, my love of the sport that kept drawing me back, but God had another reason for instilling within me a passion for the relay race. He had something important he wanted me to see.

This time, I was in America with Nick and our girls. We joined the 219.4 million Americans tuning in to the NBC coverage. On Friday, August 10, 2012, eight countries—thirty-two runners—once again took their places. Team USA was in lane 7, and my heart was right there with them.

I knew that the USA runners were at the top of their game. Tianna Madison, Allyson Felix, Bianca Knight, and Carmelita Jeter had nailed the qualifying round at the stunning speed of 41.64 seconds.[3] This time I knew that did not mean victory was secure. Bitter experience had taught me a few things:

- Having the fastest runner doesn't necessarily win the race.
- Having the fastest team doesn't necessarily win the race.
- Having the most experienced or the most dedicated runners doesn't necessarily win the race.
- Having the reigning champions or the contenders determined to reclaim their championship doesn't necessarily win the race.

Unless the baton is safely passed in each and every exchange zone and carried first across the finish line, the entire team loses.

Everything hinges on what happens in the exchange zone.

And that's when it hit me—this lesson from God twelve years in the making.

I wasn't just watching an Olympic race. I was seeing a crystal-clear representation of how the church must work and what happens when it doesn't. As those athletes moved into position in London in 2012, I was seeing the church lined up in lanes all over the globe, batons in hand, running the race that matters most in this world—the divine relay!

This divine relay is filled with exchange zones. If the baton of faith passes from person to person, from generation to generation, we speed unstoppable toward the finish line. But if the exchange is fumbled, the whole team, the whole church, suffers.

By this time in my life, I'd been traveling across the globe for years doing ministry. Nick and I had been serving the local church and leaders through Equip & Empower Ministries and then through The A21 Campaign—an organization we founded in 2008 dedicated to abolishing modern-day slavery. Our focus was on stopping human trafficking. Through Equip & Empower, as well as The A21 Campaign, I was learning just how important it is to get the "exchange zone" right to ensure that no runners stop running and walk off the field.

I'd been running the race God called me to run. I'd been handed quite a few batons along the way and had released many, some smoothly, some not so well. I had many batons I needed to deliver to the next runners. How could I do it with excellence? The divine relay is tough. There are so many ways to mangle the exchange zones, to overshoot, to be knocked off the track, to drop the baton, to stop running.

As the camera scanned the crowd that filled the Olympic stadium that day, Hebrews 12:1–2 flew into my mind:

> *Therefore, since we are surrounded by such a great cloud of witnesses, let us throw off everything that hinders and the sin that so easily entangles. And let us run with perseverance the race marked out for us, fixing our eyes on Jesus, the pioneer and perfecter of faith.*

The first verse describes a great cloud of witnesses. I considered the millions of people watching the 2012 games all over the globe. Did this compare with "a great cloud of witnesses"?

Not hardly.

Not compared to eternity! Not compared to the countless believers who have come before us and who will come after us. This was but a glimpse, a shadow, of how great God's cloud of witnesses really is.

I turned my focus back to the London 2012 games unfolding before me. Team USA was in lane 7.

The start was brilliant. It was clear by the end of the first exchange that both Jamaica and USA had the speed to take the race. Coming out of the second exchange, the USA team was firmly in the lead.

And then the magic began.

The USA lead grew. And it grew more. The third exchange was perfect, and the crowd was going wild. The USA team was flying ahead. Barring some catastrophe, the question was no longer *who* would win. The question now was this: Would the USA beat the world record?

Nick and I and the girls were on our feet cheering them on.

And we watched it happen. Team USA sailed across the finish line in a world-record-smashing 40.82 seconds! The stadium exploded in uproarious celebration. I was jumping so high my daughters thought I would hit the ceiling. We'd seen a unified team pass the baton with perfect precision and carry it first across the finish line faster than any team in history!

Perfect collaboration, each runner doing her

personal best, running in sync, reaching, receiving, releasing, and pressing on with every ounce of strength she had to give. And when the anchor runner crossed the finish line, she carried not only the baton—she carried her entire team, her entire nation, to the gold.

I love the quote from Tianna Madison, the USA starter that day. "I knew that the Olympic record was coming down," she said. "I just knew that if we had clean baton passes that we would challenge the world record. Smash it like we did? I had no idea. But I knew it was in us."

Wow. Did you catch her phrase "if we had clean baton passes"? Everything hinges on what happens in the exchange zone.

"I knew it was in us," Tianna declared.

I know it's "in us" to do the same! We can run our part in the divine relay.

Why? Because God is *in* us. God is *for* us. He tells us so in the book of Romans:

> *Those he predestined, he also called; those he called, he also justified; those he justified, he also glorified. What, then, shall we say in response to these things? If God is for us, who can be against us?*
>
> Romans 8:30–31

Our great God has not left us on our own to muddle through our spiritual exchange zones untrained. His Word and his story, written into you and me and into the lives of all believers the world over, will train us to master our exchange zones and win the race.

The race marked out for *us*.

The race marked out for *you*.

YOUR RACE

Uh-oh. It just got personal, didn't it?

God works that way.

Maybe you are just like me. I settled in to watch a great Olympic race, and the next thing I knew, *WHAM*. All the lights and cameras and eyeballs seemed to swivel from the track to focus squarely on me—on *my* race, *my* baton, *my* exchange zones.

If you are tempted to question your role in this race out of fear, a sense of inadequacy, or the impression that you've already put in your time and it's someone else's race now, think again.

God has plucked you out of eternity, positioned you in time, and given you gifts and talents to serve him in *this* generation. Your race is now. This is your time in history. You've been handed the baton of faith and entrusted to carry it forward as you run your part in God's divine relay.

Every believer is called to run, and the only spectators are those already in heaven's grandstand. Our race covers all the earth. It started before we got here and will continue after we are gone.

Perhaps you are already running your race.

Have you run out of steam? Are you winded or limping? Don't give up. Keep moving forward.

Have you dropped your baton? Don't walk off the field! You have not been disqualified.

Have you stumbled or fallen? Have you hit daunting obstacles? Do not stop! Why? Because the Christian life isn't a one-person race. It's a relay.

There is one thing you are responsible for. Only one thing matters: *Run the race marked out for you.* Run forward toward the finish line with every ounce of strength in you and with your eyes fixed on Jesus, so that you too can one day say:

> *I have fought the good fight, I have finished the race, I have kept the faith.*
> 2 Timothy 4:7

✌ TWO ✌

IMPOSSIBLE IS GOD'S STARTING POINT

Kalli's cell phone startled her awake at 3:00 a.m.

"Hello. A21. This is Kalli."

"I have escaped from the house! I ran away!" the frantic voice of a young woman cried into the phone. "I am hiding. Please come and get me!"

The young woman's broken Greek told Kalli that this victim, like most of the trafficked girls Kalli worked with through The A21 Campaign, had been brought to Kalli's town of Thessaloniki, Greece, from another country.

"We will help you," Kalli assured her. "What is your name? Where are you?"

"Katja. I am Katja. Come get me fast, please. They must know by now that I am gone and if they find me, they will kill me. They will *kill* me!" The panic in Katja's voice had Kalli's heart racing. *What horrors has this girl been through? God, help me help her*, Kalli silently prayed.

"I remember you, Katja," Kalli said, "We met just two days ago, right? I am so glad you kept my number. I will call my team and get someone to you right away. We will keep you safe. Take a deep breath and tell me where you are."

Katja described her location. It sounded as if she was well hidden at the moment, and she saw no evidence that the traffickers were nearby.

"Lord, hide Katja in the shelter of your wings until we arrive," Kalli prayed aloud. This wasn't the first time Kalli had received a panicked call from a young woman whose life was in danger.

"Katja, my team will come right away. But first I must hang up to call them. Can I do that? I will call you back within minutes. Is it okay to call you back at this number? Will you be able to safely answer it?"

There was a pause.

Kalli knew from experience that Katja would fear she was being deceived. Each of the rescued girls found it hard to trust. Who could blame them? Trust had brought most of them to Greece, and that trust had been betrayed. Many of the girls had been promised jobs or education by people they trusted, people they believed to be friends or legitimate recruiters. Most had been told that if they left their homes, paid their money, and traveled with these recruiters to Greece, jobs and other opportunities awaited them. Yet on their arrival, their papers had been taken from them and they'd been brutally beaten and repeatedly raped, threatened with death or the deaths of their families back home, and imprisoned by well-organized traffickers who forced them into prostitution.

"How do I know," Katja's now suspicious voice asked the question Kalli anticipated, "that you will come and take me to safety? How do I know you will not sell me?"

"Katja, you can trust me. I am part of A21. This is what we do. We help girls like you. You met me. You must have trusted me enough to call. Trust me now. Let me hang up and send someone to get you, and I will call you back and help bring you to safety. I promise."

"Yes. But please hurry." Katja hung up.

Lord, you've brought Katja this far. Help us reach her in time! Kalli prayed.

Kalli was running her race, passionately doing her part on the front lines of a brutal war waged by organized crime.

Kalli was ready. But she remembered well when she hadn't felt ready at all. Three years earlier, Kalli thought it was impossible for her to make a difference in the daunting evil of human trafficking. But this day, knowing that helping Katja meant endangering her own life and the lives of her teammates, Kalli was ready to run this leg of the race marked out for her.

ARE YOU READY TO RUN?

Ready is a tricky word when it comes to following God and doing his will.

Did Moses feel ready to return to Egypt and tell Pharaoh to let his people go? No. It seemed an impossible mission. Did Gideon feel ready to go strike down the Midianites and save Israel? No. Did Jeremiah feel ready to be a prophet to the nations? No. Did young Mary, a virgin teenager, feel ready to carry the Son of God in her womb? No. God's Word records the accounts of their questions, protests, reservations, and pleas demonstrating that they didn't feel ready.[1]

We can go through the Bible page by page and find person after person who didn't *feel* ready to do what God called them to do. But God didn't ask them whether they *felt* ready.

We can be certain of this: when God calls us and sends us, we *are* ready, whether we feel we are or not.

How ready are you to join the race and live in the exchange zone, arm outstretched in anticipation of the next baton God has for you?

You may be called to care for an aging parent, or to steer a troubled teen through a tumultuous time, or to lead your family through a financial crisis. You may see the need to organize a local food pantry. Perhaps a neighbor is caught in an abusive relationship and needs your help, or a spouse is suffering from depression, or the local elementary school has appealed for after-school mentors for children who have no one at home to read to them or help them with their homework. Or maybe you went to visit a loved one in prison and saw the loneliness and hopelessness of those who had no visitors.

God's call comes to each of us in every age and stage of life. He calls us to step out of our comfort zone and into the exchange zone.

Are you ready and willing to run *your* race in the divine relay?

God knew Kalli was ready to run her part in the divine relay.

How do I know? Because while I was running *my* race, God placed Kalli in the exchange zone in *my* lane, in A21, and I knew that I was to pass the baton—responsibilities to be carried out at our Thessaloniki safe house—to her.

But before she stepped into the exchange zone at the age of forty-one, Kalli, a homemaker and mother of two children, assumed it was impossible for God to use her to save lives. "I'd been a Christian for about eighteen years, attending church, growing in my faith," Kalli said. "I'd been invited by a friend to attend a Christian women's conference. There I heard Christine tell how God had recently called her into the fight against human trafficking, leading her and her husband, Nick, to start A21. The numbers she revealed were staggering."

They still are. Billions of dollars exchange hands every year in this barbaric business, largely controlled by organized crime around the globe.[2] About 800,000 people are trafficked across international borders every year, and 99 percent of those people never escape.[3]

But I'm only one woman, Kalli thought, *a mom with two kids of my own. What can I do about this massive global problem?*

"I couldn't imagine how I could make a difference, but I sensed God telling me, 'Kalli, you have a part to play in A21.' I knew I couldn't walk away. So, I signed up as a volunteer.

"I had been running in the A21 'volunteer's lane' for a while when another baton was passed to me: to come on staff as the shelter manager," Kalli recalled.

Kalli reached out and grasped that baton as well. Because of that, Kalli had met Katja a few days before that 3:00 a.m. phone call and offered her phone number.

Impossible for Kalli, a mom and homemaker, to make a difference? Tell that to Katja. When her life hung in the balance, it was Kalli she called. Then a driver came and took her to safety. A home was provided where Katja learned to heal. An officer arrested her traffickers. A lawyer won their convictions. Do you see? Today, Katja is a free woman back in her home country, attending a university because an entire team stood ready, hands outstretched, positioned at the right time and the right place to run their parts in the race.

Each of these individuals had at one time believed it was impossible for them to make a difference in a global problem. But they've discovered that together, with each of them carrying their own unique batons, they are unstoppable in carrying out God's plan.

It sounds impossible.

Fantastic! *Impossible is God's starting point.*

WHAT HOLDS YOU BACK?

Because our God is God of the impossible, the seemingly impossible can't hold us back from achieving God's purposes for us. But other things can.

So allow me to ask a personal question: What holds you back?

Anything?

Here is why I ask. I travel the globe talking with Christians in every walk of life and every phase of Christian maturity.

- Some are new believers eager to run but not sure how to get started.
- Others are burned out from living a self-focused Christian life.
- Some feel the established church has lost its relevance, but they themselves long to be relevant in the world, to make a difference.
- Most long for a taste of God's power and presence unlike anything they've ever known.
- Many believe they are not qualified or gifted enough to be used by God in big ways.

Did you find yourself in this list? Here's the good news:

God has an eternal purpose for the whole body of Christ and a divinely chosen part for every single believer.

That includes you, my friend. If you seek God's will, if you offer yourself to run his race, he will equip you to join or return to the race, no matter how impossible that may seem. Never underestimate how huge, how mighty, how world-changing and eternity-altering this divine relay really is.

When you step forward, willing to join the race and run, you, will see that the seemingly impossible isn't impossible at all. God has empowered you with his very own Holy Spirit to run to win.

Just the other day Kalli wrote, "For me, A21 is not a

job—it is my passion! It is my life! I love every moment of it, even the most challenging parts. I never in my wildest dreams imagined that I would play a part in saving lives. I am so honored to be where I am today."

If you don't have a spiritual passion burning inside you today, challenging you, leaving you wowed and honored to be doing your work for the Lord, you're missing the thrill of running your part in the race. If that's the case, then please work through this book with a seeking, open heart and an outstretched, open hand.

Don't even wait for the end of the book. Pray now!

Oh Lord, sign me up for my part in the divine relay. Start with my "impossible." Place me in my lane, in my position, in my exchange zone. Lord, I reach out, palm open, to receive the baton you have for me. Fuel me with your passion, Lord, and I will run!

Amen?

Amen!

DECISION TIME

If you just prayed that prayer with me and are awaiting your first baton—or if you've been running for a while and have a baton in hand or are waiting for the next one—here are a few questions to help you in the exchange zone.

- Why do I hold back from running my race with 100 percent commitment?
- Why do I sometimes fail to receive the baton that God holds out to me?
- What do I do with my reluctance to release the baton—given that, when I depend on others, they sometimes let me down or fail me?
- What makes me fumble the exchange or drop the baton? And if I do, what then?
- What happens if I run off course, and how can I find my way back?
- What is it that tempts me to quit the race altogether?
- The race is sometimes long and hard. Why does my passion sometimes wither away, and what can I do to refuel it?
- What can I do to run better, smarter, and stronger?

News flash: We don't have to look any further than our own neighborhoods or even our own homes to find the glaring needs of our broken world. Yet somehow, far too many of us reason this way: I don't know where my calling is. I don't feel led. Not yet.

I confess, I get a little over-the-top passionate in my answer to that, but here it is:

WAKE UP, CHRISTIAN!

God's Word calls you. Let God's Word lead you.

This is why it is said:
    "Wake up, sleeper,
    rise from the dead,
    and Christ will shine on you."
Be very careful, then, how you live—not as unwise
but as wise, making the most of every opportunity,
because the days are evil.

Ephesians 5:14–16

Always give yourselves fully to the work of the
Lord, because you know that your labor in the
Lord is not in vain.

1 Corinthians 15:58

Do you want to find your place? Do you want to know your part?

Do something.

Do anything.

But don't just stand there.

Run!

Pray. Fast. Find a need that needs filling and fill it. Find others who are running and run with them.

God Almighty, who calls you by name, wants to make you a partner in his eternal work.

When you run your race, you will see the impossible

melt away as God's power is unleashed in you and through you to a broken world. God's plans for your eternal impact on this world are beyond your wildest imagination.

Sound impossible? Of course it is!

But impossible is God's starting point.

Jesus looked at them and said, "With man this is impossible, but with God all things are possible."
Matthew 19:26

THREE

FULLY QUALIFIED FOR YOUR RACE

You want to hear about impossible?

Kalli grew up in South Africa. Rejected by her mother as a child, Kalli was sexually and physically abused for many years, which eventually led, at the age of eighteen, to her accepting a job in her city of Cape Town as an escort for her company's clients, understanding full well that providing sex was part of her job. And guess what her father did for a living? He was part of the Mafia in South Africa—a drug dealer, a nightclub owner, and a trafficker of humans. Haunted by childhood traumas and a broken family, starving for affection, and feeling used and worthless, Kalli sought to escape her pain through drug use.

This is the woman who answered the desperate call from Katja. I couldn't make this stuff up!

Something drastically altered the course of Kalli's life. Her father—a drug-dealing human trafficker—accepted Christ. God's call to Kalli's father, and his acceptance of that call, led him to carry the baton of faith into Kalli's life. After witnessing the radical change in her father's life, Kalli surrendered her own life to Jesus and became a Christian at the age of twenty-three.

One exchange zone led to the next, one baton to the next, and so she was running in the exchange zone when, at the age of forty-one, she reached out and grasped the A21 baton.

Now let's step back and consider the one who brought the gospel to Kalli's father. We don't know his name, but God does. And there was someone who carried the gospel to that person, and the person before. Do you see how the divine relay stretches back?

And now Katja—a once broken and abused sex slave—is running her own race, carrying on the baton. Katja is one of many girls who've been helped through Kalli's work at A21. Some are now carrying their batons in Greece. Others are in Bulgaria, Nigeria, the US, Australia, South Africa, the UK, Norway, Ukraine, and Asia.

Do you see how the divine relay stretches forward? Are you beginning to get the picture of how big, how huge, how interconnected and unstoppable it is? God's

Word describes the ongoing nature of the divine relay, touching generation after generation with these words:

> *One generation commends your works to another;*
> *they tell of your mighty acts....*
> *All your works praise you, Lord;*
> *your faithful people extol you.*
> *They tell of the glory of your kingdom*
> *and speak of your might,*
> *so that all people may know of your mighty acts*
> *and the glorious splendor of your kingdom.*
> *Your kingdom is an everlasting kingdom,*
> *and your dominion endures through all generations.*
> Psalm 145:4, 10–13

THE MULTIPLICATION FACTOR

When we move into the exchange zone, God multiplies our efforts. This divine multiplication factor is critically important for us to understand. All too often, rather than seeing ourselves as qualified by God to play a great part in his race, we look at our lives—our limitations, our meager resources, our brokenness, our apparent insignificance in this huge world—and we feel unqualified to be used mightily by God, and so we slink to the sidelines.

It is heartbreaking for me to meet Christians who

love the Lord and desire to serve him, but who shy away from playing their part because they don't understand God's divine multiplication factor. "After all," they reason, "I'm just one person. My involvement isn't going to make a dent in what's wrong in this world. I'm not qualified enough for God to use me in important ways."

That kind of thinking would have stopped the man in South Africa from witnessing to the drug-dealing human-trafficker who was Kalli's father. Do you see the potential ripple effects when just one person walks away from his or her exchange zone?

Of course we are small, but God is huge.

Of course we have limitations, but God is limitless.

Of course we are weak, but God is strong.

Of course we are finite, but God is infinite.

Of course we are imperfect, but God is perfect.

Of course we fail, but God never fails.

God calls you to step into the exchange zone not because *you* are mighty and strong. He calls you to take your place in the race because *he* is mighty and strong!

HOW NOT ENOUGH BECOMES MORE THAN ENOUGH

Some two thousand years ago, on a hillside swarming with thousands of hungry people, the disciples found themselves confronted with a problem that looked too big to overcome.

Jesus had been teaching and healing a large crowd all day.[1] His words were so life-giving, so earth-shattering, that they stayed hour after hour after hour to hear more. Late in the day, the disciples came to Jesus, saying he should send the people away so they could go to surrounding villages and buy themselves something to eat.

So Jesus asks, "How many loaves do you have?"

Andrew, one of the disciples, comes back with, "Here is a boy with five small barley loaves and two small fish, but how far will they go among so many?" Notice that Andrew didn't just say it was five barley loaves and two fish. He called them *small* loaves and *small* fish.

Notice that Jesus asks them how much there is to go around. He makes sure that the disciples recognize the limitations they are facing. Until we hit our limit, we often assume we can provide, we can deliver, and we can produce.

What are you facing today that brings you face-to-face with your limitations? We must never assess a difficulty in light of our own resources but in light of God's resources because *God's resources are limitless.* Jesus accepted the five loaves and two fishes, small though they were. One packed lunch. A meager amount of food. If the boy had kept his little lunch, it would have remained little. If you keep your little, it will remain little as well.

I love this next part! Do you know the first thing Jesus did with that meager offering? He looked up to heaven and gave thanks to God for the little he was given by the boy. I wonder what it was like for that boy to see his meager meal held up to the heavens by the hands of a grateful Jesus. Jesus, of course, knew it wasn't going to remain little, that it was about to be multiplied into great abundance. But let's not miss this moment. The Son of God, holding our offering up to Almighty God and blessing it with his thanks! Always remember that *God celebrates our gifts to him and blesses them.*

Next, Jesus broke the bread and the fish. When he blessed it, there were five and two. But when he broke it, we lose count. The more he broke the bread and fish, the more there was to feed and nourish. The disciples started distributing the food, and soon what was broken was feeding thousands. *The miracle is in the breaking.* It is in the breaking that God multiplies not enough into more than enough.

Are there broken places in your life so painful that you fear the breaking will destroy you? Did you have a broken marriage? Did you have a broken past? Have you experienced brokenness in your body? Have your finances been broken? What should have disqualified Kalli from the race was the very thing that qualified her for it. *When our broken pieces are offered to God, he multiplies them for his purposes.*

Listen to what Jesus said when everyone had been filled and satisfied:

> *He said to his disciples, "Gather the pieces that are left over. Let nothing be wasted."*
> John 6:12

"Let nothing be wasted." The next time you are tempted to withhold your contribution to the kingdom, believing it to be too small or too broken to make a difference, don't forget that not only will God celebrate, bless, and multiply your contribution, he will also value every little bit of it. *God never wastes what we offer to him.*

All four of the disciples who wrote the Gospels—Matthew, Mark, Luke, and John—record this miraculous hillside feeding, and all report the number of people fed as five thousand men, which did not include the women and children. Matthew 14:21 makes that very clear: "The number of those who ate was about five thousand men, besides women and children."

Have you ever noticed that part of the verse? I used to think, *Why didn't they count everybody? Why only the men?* Until a powerful realization occurred to me.

Whose lunch was it that Jesus multiplied? It was a child who gave his meager lunch—an *uncounted* boy!

The disciples did not count the very one whom God had moved into position to release his miracle.

Isn't that just like God to use people whom other people do not count?

As a mom, I like to think about that boy's mama who packed his lunch that day. She didn't know she was packing the ingredients for a miracle, did she?

God is not waiting for you, hoping you'll eventually bring him extraordinary talents, abilities, accomplishments, and gifts. The time is now to give him what you have, no matter how ordinary or insignificant it seems. In the divine relay, *God uses the ordinary to do the extraordinary.*

GREAT EXPECTATIONS

Be confident that God will take your little and make it much.

Are your resources too limited to change the world? Great. His resources are limitless. Do you not have enough to offer him? No problem. God multiplies your not enough into more than enough.

Are you broken, thinking you are too wounded to be qualified to serve? The miracle is in the breaking. What has been broken, God is able to multiply for his purposes.

Do you feel so used up and worn down that all you have left to offer are your leftovers? Marvelous. God values your leftovers and never wastes one morsel of what you have to offer.

Do you believe you are too insignificant to count in carrying batons that will change this world and have an eternal impact? The uncounted count. God counts on you doing your part.

Are you so ordinary that you have no remarkable gifts or talents for God to use? How wonderful! God uses the ordinary to do his extraordinary.

Congratulations! You've qualified to take your place in the exchange zone.

Each of you should use whatever gift you have received to serve others, as faithful stewards of God's grace in its various forms. If anyone speaks, they should do so as one who speaks the very words of God. If anyone serves, they should do so with the strength God provides, so that in all things God may be praised through Jesus Christ. To him be the glory and the power for ever and ever. Amen.

1 Peter 4:10–11

❧ FOUR ❧

EMBRACE YOUR PLACE

I was twenty-two years old and had been volunteering at the youth center for several months, serving food to hurting and broken young people, listening to their problems, and inviting them to tell me their stories. Coming here was the highlight of my week, and I loved knowing that each time I showed up, I was making a difference in the life of a lonely or wounded person.

I spotted Jeremy coming my way through the crowd. He was a regular. I didn't know his story, but he had all the telltale signs of a troubled kid in search of a place to belong.

"Jeremy," I called out to him. "Over here."

When our eyes met, I could see he was drunk.

Before I had the chance to say another word, he clutched his stomach and then projectile vomited all over the people in his path, me included.

Instinctively I delegated. As I steadied Jeremy and led him toward a chair, I turned to someone and said, "Go get some toilet paper and clean this mess up."

A moment later a few people came back, rolls of toilet paper in hand. Suddenly I felt the Holy Spirit saying to me, "Christine, you wipe up the vomit."

I have an extreme aversion to vomit, even to this day with my own children. But I reached for a roll of toilet paper and began wiping the vomit off of Jeremy's chin and jacket and shirt. As I did, I sensed the Holy Spirit impressing on my heart, "Christine, this is what you're going to spend your life doing—wiping up the vomit of a lost and broken generation."

I was so new to running in the divine relay that hearing from God in such a powerful way made me tremble with awe. I was on holy ground. This messy work was his holy work.

God was giving me my first lesson in a critically important principle: In order to thrive in the exchange zone, we must learn to *embrace our place*. To embrace your place means that wherever you are in life, you see yourself as an important member of God's divine relay.

In principle, that sounds simple, doesn't it? But in

reality—in those covered-in-vomit kinds of moments—
it is all too easy for us to miss the opportunities to
embrace our place.

ONE TEAM, MANY RUNNERS

No one denomination, tradition, tribe, or church displays all of God's greatness any more than one star
reflects all the glory of God.

To help us understand this mystery, God chose the
image of the human body.

> *Now you are the body of Christ, and each one of*
> *you is a part of it.*
> 1 Corinthians 12:27

God calls us the body of Christ, and he chooses
to be represented on this earth through us, his body.
People see God at work on the earth through his
church. The body of Christ is the visible representation
of an invisible God to our friends, our neighbors, and
the world. The more connected, interdependent, and
unified we are, the more of God the world sees through
the work of his church. Look at this next passage and
ask yourself how it applies to you as you run your part
in God's divine relay.

*Just as a body, though one, has many parts, but all
its many parts form one body, so it is with Christ.
For we were all baptized by one Spirit so as to
form one body—whether Jews or Gentiles, slave
or free—and we were all given the one Spirit to
drink. Even so the body is not made up of one part
but of many.*

1 Corinthians 12:12–14

DISPLACED OR MISPLACED

If we are going to run this race well, we must each
learn to embrace our place. Have you found yourself
mystified, frustrated, or discouraged when the reality
of playing your part in serving God falls short of your
expectations?

Let's take the time to recognize a few common
causes of feeling displaced or misplaced.

OBSCURITY AND ANONYMITY

Many believers feel stuck behind the scenes. Some
begin doing God's work with the hope of making a
difference but then discover that such work is messy,
smelly, unglamorous, and tedious. "Is this what I came
for?" they might ask. "Surely God has bigger, more
important work for me to do."

CIRCUMSTANCES AND TRIALS

I also speak to many whose challenges are coming from circumstances that thwart their efforts to do what they believe they've been called to do. Maybe a permit falls through on the expansion of a ministry center, or a woman teaching a thriving neighborhood Bible study is struck down with cancer, or a man leading an effective prison ministry loses his job and must relocate in order to support his family. The list is endless.

PROMOTION AND TIMING

If I have learned one thing in ministry, it is that most God dreams take longer than we think to realize, cost more than we ever thought we would have to pay, and are far more painful to birth than we ever imagined. Many start the race with high energy and vibrant passion, but when they do not move ahead as quickly as they think they should, they lose their zeal and commitment.

These common challenges lead some to make a huge mistake: they stop running their race! Some quit. Some shrink back from taking risks and serve within a comfort zone. Others quietly sit in the pew and never serve again, focusing on their own private spiritual needs but missing out on the rewards of running the race marked out for them.

God not only has a place for each one of us, he also

has perfect timing when it comes to moving us from one position to the next. If you leave the race, you will be disconnected from the very purposes God has in mind for you. If you try to transplant yourself to the place you want to be, you may find yourself even more frustrated or ineffective.

But if you stay faithful in your pursuit of God and learn to embrace your place, then his work in and through you will be unstoppable.

GOD CHOOSES THE PART WE PLAY

I don't know what your story is, where you've been, what you've done, or what has been done to you. But I do know from God's Word that you are not here, in this place and this time, by accident. As you give God your time, your gifts, your resources and talents, he will use them to have a critically important and eternal impact on this world.

God demonstrates this truth in the story of David when he was anointed the next king of Israel.

Saul was the first king of the Israelites, but after leading them for about twenty-five years, Saul rebelled so much against the Lord that God sent his prophet Samuel to anoint the future king who would succeed Saul.[1]

> *The Lord said to Samuel ... "I am sending you to*
> *Jesse of Bethlehem. I have chosen one of his sons to*
> *be king."*
>
> 1 Samuel 16:1

So Samuel went as instructed and had Jesse present his sons. We are about to witness an important principle: *God chooses the part we play.* Let's admit it—from a human standpoint, there are times when God's choices defy our logic. Left to his own judgment, the prophet got it wrong. He looked at the firstborn, Eliab, saw his impressive appearance and size, and assumed Eliab must be God's choice.

> *When they arrived, Samuel saw Eliab and*
> *thought, "Surely the Lord's anointed stands here*
> *before the Lord."*
> *But the Lord said to Samuel, "Do not consider*
> *his appearance or his height, for I have rejected*
> *him. The Lord does not look at the things people*
> *look at. People look at the outward appearance, but*
> *the Lord looks at the heart."*
>
> 1 Samuel 16:6–7

So Samuel considered the next son, and then the next, and the one after that, until finally,

Jesse had seven of his sons pass before Samuel, but Samuel said to him, "The Lord has not chosen these." So he asked Jesse, "Are these all the sons you have?"

"There is still the youngest," Jesse answered. "He is tending the sheep."

1 Samuel 16:10–11

David, the last born, the least qualified from a human point of view, was so far removed from his father's mind as a possible candidate for this job that Jesse hadn't even brought him to the selection process. We can hardly imagine his shock when, plucked from his shepherding, he found himself face-to-face with a prophet of God who did this:

Then the Lord said, "Rise and anoint him; this is the one."

So Samuel took the horn of oil and anointed him in the presence of his brothers, and from that day on the Spirit of the Lord came powerfully upon David.

1 Samuel 16:12–13

David did not choose to be king. God chose David to be king.

And where was David when he was summoned? Serving in obscurity.

Are you given the jobs that no one else wants? Welcome them. Do you feel disregarded by your family, your boss, your coworkers? Then you are in David's good company.

GOD PREPARES THOSE HE CHOOSES

Anyone can, in a matter of moments, snap a picture and upload it for instant viewing across the globe. But back in my day, when dinosaurs roamed the earth, photos were developed in a darkroom. The process took time and care. If someone opened the darkroom door and let in too much light or tried to take shortcuts in the development process, the images would be destroyed.

In the same way, to fulfill God's purpose for our lives, we must commit to the process of God's darkroom. God uses time, circumstances, and trials to burn the light of Christ into our souls so that when we emerge from his darkroom, nothing can destroy the image of his Son developed in our lives.

We see this in David's life. Neither Samuel nor David had any inkling of when David would take the throne. *Just because David had been anointed with a divine purpose did not mean it was his appointed time.*

David did not yet have the skill, wisdom, or knowledge to lead the nation. He was anointed, but his character and spirit needed to be developed, and that would require that he follow and obey God every step of the way along what would prove to be a long, mystifying, and difficult journey.

I didn't have a clue that God's work would take me from a local youth center to a national youth ministry, then to a global church ministry, and then on to be one of God's warriors in the fight against the injustice of human slavery. I never imagined that God would use an adopted, abused, marginalized, immigrant female to open rescue homes for women sold as sex slaves around the world and to hire lawyers to win convictions of the organized criminals exploiting those women.

But I can see now that I didn't need to know any of that. All I needed to do was embrace the place God had for me that day in the youth center, wiping Jeremy's vomit off him, off myself, and off the floor.

David embraced his place. He became an armor-bearer to Saul. Assuming the posture of a servant was his training ground to be a king. He was the errand boy in battle, willingly carrying lunch to his brothers. Even though they'd seen him anointed, he did not seek to lord it over them. It was there, as David delivered lunches—a seemingly unimportant act of service—that he heard for himself the taunts of the giant, Goliath.

Had David not spent years protecting his sheep from predators, had he not been learning and meditating on the Scriptures, he would not have had the strength or the courage to take out the giant.

Are you seeing how God works? There is a process— a divine order—that requires submission first, and only then our gradual promotion. *God requires our obedience before our understanding.*

GOD PROMOTES IN HIS PERFECT TIMING

Because David persevered, because he was faithful each step of the way, because he did not give up, in God's perfect timing he became king.

> *David was thirty years old when he became king, and he reigned forty years.*
> 2 Samuel 5:4

David endured many injustices, dangers, and hardships until God's image was so fused to David's soul that we still see it today in his story and his writings.

David embraced his place. Do you know the ultimate plans God had for him? Not only did David become the greatest king of Israel, not only did he pen some of the most eloquent and beloved words of Scripture, but he also was in the lineage of Jesus Christ.

Do we trust God to do in his own timing what only he can do?

This is exactly what God is asking of you. This trust enables you to say:

"Yes, Lord, I will fight for the survival of this difficult marriage."

"Yes, I will remain honest through this bad financial situation."

"Yes, I will continue to serve in this ministry through every challenge."

"Yes, I will love my child selflessly, even when I am despised for it."

"Yes, I will take the high road and offer forgiveness in this broken relationship."

This is living in obedience before understanding. This kind of trust grows when you embrace your place.

GO WITH WHAT YOU KNOW

Where are you right now in embracing your place? Whether you are eighteen or eighty, you don't yet know the full story of what God plans to accomplish *through* you in this world. But you do know what he plans to accomplish *in* you. He plans to make you more and more like Jesus.

In trust and obedience, go with what you *do* know rather than fret over what you *don't* know. Love God. Obey him. Trust him. Serve him.

Will you trust God enough to embrace your place? Then pray now.

God, I trust you. No matter what happens, I believe that you are at work for my eternal best and my part in your kingdom. Even when I can't see it or understand it, I believe it. I offer you my obedience no matter what I encounter. Do whatever it takes, Lord, to prepare me for the future you have in mind for me. Amen.

Rejoice! God is building his strength and character in you, growing your capacity to carry greater batons, one after another, into a future you have not yet imagined, across a finish line that, though still shrouded in fog, God describes in this way:

> *"I know the plans I have for you," declares the Lord, "plans to prosper you and not to harm you, plans to give you hope and a future."*
> Jeremiah 29:11

FIVE

NEVER STAND STILL IN THE EXCHANGE ZONE

Kristen drew a steadying breath as she stepped into the prestigious Cecil B. Day Chapel of the Carter Center in Atlanta. Everything about this room—the two tiers of cushioned chairs, the highly polished wood trim accenting the walls and stately columns, the whispered hush of perfect acoustics—created an aura of official dignity.

She would soon step onto that stage to address more than three hundred people—professional educators, various law enforcement personnel, FBI agents, first responders, political and community leaders, and journalists. This conference, hosted by the Georgia

Department of Education, had been called to discuss the impact of human trafficking on the students of Georgia and to explore how the schools and community could join the fight against it.

Every one of these attendees and presenters is at least twice my age, Kristen thought. *Lord, every doubt and insecurity inside of me is screaming for me to run home*, Kristen prayed. *I am stepping out in obedience, knowing you have sent me here and promised to go with me.* She suddenly felt a calm pour over her and smiled at the memory of her A21 teammates gathered around her, praying for this day. She knew they were praying at this very moment.

One by one, presenters took the stage to shed light on child sex trafficking, emphasizing that it wasn't only an international problem but a local one. She heard the estimates that every single month, more than four hundred children, both internationals and locals, were trafficked in Georgia. This shocked many in the audience. But nothing she heard surprised her.

She checked the time on her muted cell phone, then stood and slipped up the aisle to await her cue to move onto the stage.

Kristen shared the story of how she had joined the battle against human trafficking when she first learned that girls like her were being sold as slaves around the world. She gave the testimonies of several women who'd been rescued through the work of The A21 Campaign and then presented the curriculum A21 was developing for use in high schools around the world. Her heart soared as she watched the audience taking copious notes and nodding with surprise as they listened. God was using her!

After her presentation, the attendees sought her out, eager to hear more. She distributed copies of the curriculum under development and gathered valuable feedback from many educators. Near the end of the conference, her jaw dropped when the Georgia Department of Education announced they would use the A21 curriculum in a pilot program in Georgia high schools.

THE VEIL IS LIFTED

That day, the veil was lifted just a bit for Kristen as she caught a glimpse of the sheer magnitude of the divine relay and her part in it. There were more lanes than she'd known. More runners than she'd imagined. God was on the move. He had propelled her into this life-saving work to play a part in his plan.

As Kristen headed home from the conference, she thought back six years earlier to when another veil had been lifted—the day when she'd first heard the shocking reality of modern-day human trafficking.

Kristen is a perfect example of another principle in

becoming an unstoppable runner in God's relay: *Never stand still in the exchange zone.* I've learned in my relay to hand batons *only* to those who are already running.

When Kristen heard of the need to help save young women from the horror of trafficking, she felt moved to take action, to do something, *anything*, to help. So this tenderhearted teen returned to her friends at Hudsonville High School in Michigan and shared not only the tragic news of human trafficking but also the A21 plans to open the first ever safe house in Greece. *She saw a need and set out to meet it. She dreamed big, dove in, and reached out to others to join her.* Her high school friends were so inspired by her passion that they went to work dreaming up ways to raise awareness and funds for the cause.

Under Kristen's leadership, they sponsored a walkathon in their town, challenged local schools to a "change war" to see who could collect the most spare change for the cause, and organized a battle of the bands among students. Motivated by the students' passion, their school officials and church youth leaders joined in, offering to dye their hair pink or shave their heads if the kids hit their goals—which they did!

Yes, Kristen ran. She was off in Michigan running laps and passing batons before we'd ever heard her name.

As she ran, she grew. She learned how to assemble a team, how to cast vision, how to find her way around challenges and learn from mistakes as well as from success.

During that time, Kristen connected by email with Annie, one of the original A21 team members. Annie encouraged Kristen in her efforts and reported them back to the rest of our team. We were overjoyed that a sixteen-year-old had taken it upon herself to start running in the race to abolish this evil. This little band of high school friends collected $32,000 and sent it to us to help get the rescue house in Greece off the ground. Can you believe that?

ON-THE-JOB TRAINING

Because Kristen chose to run in the exchange zone rather than stand still, Annie and I saw Kristen in the race. So when we had a baton to pass along, we ran into Kristen's exchange zone and offered her the baton of an internship with A21 as she neared high school graduation.

However, Kristen had also been offered a full-ride college scholarship. She had a choice to make. "I knew that I could take either path and God would still have me involved in his kingdom work," Kristen explained. "Either way, I would be blessed and able to touch people's lives and make a difference. But I felt an urge, a call, to join The A21 Campaign. Deep down I knew that by working for A21, it would be more about who I was becoming than what I was going to accomplish."

She had that right! How is that for moving into the future God has for you? Kristen had two good lanes to choose from, but knew that to run the race she was made for, she had to choose one and turn away from the other. She chose the one that she believed would most stretch her spiritual life.

We had the privilege of watching her grow. She ran well. She was faithful with every baton given to her, even batons such as managing the back end of our website for a season. Despite her inexperience and lack of a "calling" to website work, Kristen embraced her place. She accepted every responsibility she was given, and, as a result, she developed skills she would never have learned if she had refused to be stretched. In fact, she didn't just accept each responsibility—she owned it, and in owning it, she demonstrated willingness to tackle the tasks at hand, even those she didn't necessarily want to do. The result? Each new task strengthened her and increased her capacity, flexibility, and endurance. If you stop running because you don't like a particular aspect of your race, you will miss out on the growth that comes from being stretched beyond your comfort zone.

Kristen ran so well and increased her personal capacity so much that, three years later, we asked her to oversee the curriculum project we hoped would be used in high schools around the globe to raise awareness, prevent new victims, and stimulate new solutions to the problem. Though Kristen was not a trained educator, though she was without a college degree, though she'd never written curriculum before, *she had been running in the lane of student initiatives and growing in her ability.*

Kristen accepted the baton of directing curriculum development, and again she excelled. That led me to choose her to represent A21 at the conference in Georgia, and today, thanks to Kristen's work, God is multiplying those efforts many thousandfold in the US alone. That day when she stood on the conference stage, she tossed out batons right and left, carrying the work of God's kingdom into countless lives.

When Kristen returned home to our office in California after her presentation in Georgia, I was so proud of her I thought I would burst. She'd run well, and I knew the baton our team had handed her—to represent us at this conference—had been placed in the hand of the right runner for the job.

Today in Kristen's work at A21, she manages a team of highly qualified educators twice her age who are scattered around the world, crafting and refining the curriculum. Because she and A21 value education and professionalism, she is also a university student, learning all she can to excel even more at the work she's been called to do.

"I knew that from a human perspective, I was not qualified to be on that stage," Kristen said. "I did not have the life experience, knowledge, charisma, or education level of anyone else who spoke that day. But I do have the Holy Spirit in me who empowers me by his grace and power. I learned that day in a profound way that God is really the only qualifier we need." It is one thing to be able to quote a Scripture and an entirely different thing to live it out. In that assembly Kristen felt the reality of this Scripture verse:

> *He said to me, "My grace is sufficient for you, for my power is made perfect in weakness." Therefore I will boast all the more gladly about my weaknesses, so that Christ's power may rest on me.*
> 2 Corinthians 12:9

The Christian life is always, always on-the-job training.

WE ARE HIS HANDIWORK

In the divine relay, there is no place for idleness or procrastination. The race is on! When you are running with your hand reaching back, palm open, ready and waiting, the baton finds you. God will place it in your open hand. As long as you keep running, God is equipping you to do the work at hand, all the while preparing you in ways you've never imagined to do the next work he will call you to do.

But such growth is dependent on never growing stagnant—batons cannot pass between those who are not running.

Remember the relay in the Olympic races? The starter breaks away from the starting line. Runner number two is in the exchange zone and begins to run, then accelerates, then reaches back and runs flat-out, eyes fixed forward, never back, and keeps running until that baton is slapped into his or her hand. If the person in the exchange zone were standing still, and the race would be lost!

How did those runners win their places on the team? By running, running, and running some more. Practice increased their strength and improved their speed.

God not only powerfully uses people who are runners—"just do something" kinds of people—he trains them by keeping a steady supply of new batons flowing into their lives and thereby grows their capacity to have an impact on this world. This is what happens when we do God's work. *We develop to the level of where we need to go.*

Today Kristen laughs at the memory of her first response when I asked her to make that presentation.

"I freaked out when Chris first asked me to be the one to go present in Georgia," Kristen said. "Why me? I'd expected her to go. She'd have blown the roof off the place! I was nervous and instantly had doubts and thoughts of insecurity. But as I prayed about it, I realized it was clearly a God thing. God had placed me there for a reason. I had to choose to step out in obedience and rely on his promises to meet me there."

As long as we run with our eyes fixed on Jesus, we learn, we grow, we stretch, and we become better runners than ever before. God is always working on us and in us for our good and his glory.

Don't come to a standstill when you hit daunting challenges or new territory. Don't wait to serve, hoping to grow qualified before you take the next step. Be faithful in running, even if you, like Kristen, find yourself running into intimidating situations. Keep running, confident that God will train you as you run.

WHAT KIND OF GOD?

Kristen exemplifies the stages we've covered in these first five chapters. As a sixteen-year-old believer, she'd already committed herself to be a runner in God's divine relay and attended a conference to help her run. She didn't consider the impossibility of stopping human trafficking; she believed God could use her new knowledge as a starting point. Believing that God had qualified her to do her part, she offered herself to him, and he multiplied her efforts. She embraced the place where God had her—her local high school and youth group. She didn't sit there idle. She simply ran and, in doing so, she grew in her abilities, her skills, and her confidence, not only boldly handing off batons to others who joined the race because of her, but also finding new batons placed in her open, outstretched hand.

Kristen has it right when she says, "I don't have to be the most qualified person in the race. I just need to show up, do the part that I'm being asked to play, and then I begin to discover that I am *benefiting* from it. As I'm pouring out my efforts for God, God is pouring his life into me."

What kind of God sends a twenty-two-year-old girl with no college degree into a conference of professionals to inspire them to adopt a curriculum that she is overseeing?

The same God who sends a murderer to lead his people out of slavery (Moses), a shepherd boy to kill a giant (David), a virgin to bear a savior (Mary), a child to give his meager lunch (the uncounted boy), a common fisherman to lead his church (Peter), an unqualified Aussie to rescue modern-day slaves (me), and *you* to do his work on this earth.

Yes, you are in the very same lineup as all the other champions of the faith. God's relay is filled with willing runners who have to run from exchange zone to exchange zone, always receiving his on-the-job training for the work he has planned for us to do.

> *For we are God's handiwork, created in Christ Jesus to do good works, which God prepared in advance for us to do.*
> Ephesians 2:10

ᴄ⤵ SIX ᴄ⤵

THE MYSTERY REVEALED

I could hardly breathe for the wonder of it all.

It was a Sunday evening in January 1989 when I first stepped into what looked to me like a warehouse. I took my seat on a folding chair among several hundred people, not sure what to expect from a church so different in appearance from the traditional sanctuary I'd attended as a child. The next thing I knew, I was surrounded by the joyful sound of voices lifted in wholehearted praise. I saw faces and arms lifted to heaven; I heard the Word of God proclaimed; I heard heartfelt prayers taken to the throne of God. Whatever this was, I wanted more, and I somehow knew I'd found what I didn't even know I'd been looking for—a church family. A spiritual home.

An announcement was made that people were needed to help set up chairs one night that week, and I couldn't wait to volunteer. From then on, every time those church doors were open, I was there. If the church needed volunteers to scrub floors, wash windows, clean out closets, rearrange furniture, organize the storage room, you name it, I was there.

The church was young and vibrant and graciously reached out and welcomed everyone to join in. "Hey, if you're willing, have a go at it! Serve. Take part." You didn't have to get your life all cleaned up before you could serve. You didn't have to wait twenty years or pass a theology test to earn your place. Every service, every event, cried out to me with open arms of acceptance that seemed to say, "Come just as you are and join us in being transformed by God from the inside out."

I started a Bible-reading plan. I started to journal. I joined a small group. For the first time in my life, I developed a daily intimate relationship with the Holy Spirit of God. God's Spirit began convicting me of sin and prompting me to burn some destructive bridges to my past.

Driven by an insatiable appetite for God's truth, I listened to the week's sermons multiple times each week. Everything about the way I saw God, the world, and myself was radically changing because I was in the Word every day.

One day I read this verse in Isaiah:

Then I heard the voice of the Lord saying, "Whom shall I send? And who will go for us?" And I said, "Here am I. Send me!"
Isaiah 6:8

A deep passion stirred the core of my being. A powerful desire swept over me to go all over the world telling others of this Jesus who was radically transforming my life.

There was a mystery at work in me. I did not yet have the vocabulary to explain it. But I knew something mysterious, something glorious and wonderful, was happening inside of me.

Paul, in his letter to the Colossians, explains it beautifully.

We continually ask God to fill you with the knowledge of his will through all the wisdom and understanding that the Spirit gives, so that you may live a life worthy of the Lord and please him in every way: bearing fruit in every good work, growing in the knowledge of God.
Colossians 1:9–10

This is precisely what I was experiencing—the knowledge of God's will was infiltrating my life and I was beginning to "bear fruit," meaning that I was making a difference in the lives of others through the good work God was entrusting to my care. The Spirit of God was giving me wisdom and understanding beyond my own limited perspective as my knowledge of God—his heart, his purposes, his ways—was growing. Paul goes on a few verses later to reveal that he has been commissioned by God to reveal *a mystery*.

> *God gave me [the commission] to present to you the word of God in its fullness—the mystery that has been kept hidden for ages and generations but is now disclosed to the Lord's people. To them God has chosen to make known among the Gentiles the glorious riches of this mystery.*
> Colossians 1:25–27

What a buildup he is giving this mystery. Finally, he reveals it:

> *This mystery, which is* Christ in you, *the hope of glory.*
> Colossians 1:27, emphasis added

The something wonderful that I'd been experiencing was Christ in me.

THE MYSTERY AT WORK

Eleven months flew by. In that time, under sound teaching, and feeding on God's Word, I began to understand that all these changes I'd been experiencing were *Christ in me* reshaping my heart. During this time, I had my "embrace your place" lesson with Jeremy in the youth center. I was now running my part in God's divine relay, and as I ran, *Christ in me* was growing in the knowledge of God.

One November day, I went to the church in response to an announcement that help was needed to clean up a storeroom. I walked in to discover I was the only one who'd turned up to clean that day. I enjoy bringing order out of chaos and finished the job quickly.

As I walked out of the storeroom, the assistant youth pastor, John, was standing at the top of the stairs, and he said, "You're Christine Caryofyllis, aren't you?" (My maiden name. I told you I was Greek.)

My heart pounded. In those eleven months, I'd hardly spoken a word to any leader in the church. I'd felt like a kid just grateful to watch them from a distance.

"Um, yeah" was the most profound response I could muster.

"I've noticed you a lot. You're always around."

I beamed, shocked to learn I'd been noticed. "Yeah. I just love it here."

"You've got a degree in psychology, don't you?"

I didn't. I had just done two years of introductory psychology and was majoring in English and economic history, so I filled him in, then said, "I can read Golden Books and count to ten. That's about it."

He smiled. "Well, look, we've just gotten a government grant to start a youth center. I'm going on a mission trip with our senior pastor for a few weeks, and when I come back, I'd love you to have researched it and just find us somewhere to start the youth center."

I stood there slack-jawed.

And then a remarkable thing happened. He reached to his belt, unclipped his pager (a gadget invented long before cell phones), and, from the top of the stairs, he tossed it to me.

Instinctively my hands went up and I caught it. It looked like an ordinary pager. But do you know what it really was?

It was a baton.

I gulped. I heard myself accept the assignment, and I left the building. What did I know of government grants or running a youth center? I'd never even attended a youth ministry event until five months before. I knew nothing about the hows or whys or whats of a Christian youth center. I didn't even know my way around the Bible yet! Why had I agreed?

Thanks to the heart changes growing inside me, I didn't respond as I would have in the past. The old

Christine would have quit before she started out of the fear of failure and not being good enough. But the new Christine was willing, in spite of her fear, to step out in faith.

DISCOVERING THE POWER
OF CHRIST IN ME

The next six weeks, I was a woman with a mission. Since I didn't have a clue how to research the opening of a youth center, my daily prayer and devotional time took on a new focus: *Dear God, please show me what to do.*

This was a turning point for me. The old Christine would have relied on her own strengths and resources. But that old Christine was shrinking away as *Christ in me* was growing larger. I was now willing to admit my weakness and ask God and others for help without fear of looking foolish. I was now able to pray and believe that God would answer. I was running, openhanded, ready for God's on-the-job training. And God had just the right lesson ready for me to learn: *Rely on God's power, not your own.*

After seeking God's guidance, I looked for every community-based youth center within a twenty-mile radius and visited all of them. I asked every question I could think of about what they were doing, why, and how. I discovered that we just had to identify the practical needs of youth in our local community and then meet them.

God, you and I know I haven't got the slightest idea what I'm doing, I'd pray each morning, *so please give me your favor.* Then I'd set up meetings with Rotary clubs and local business leaders and the police department.

I discovered there was no shortage of needs, just a shortage of resources and people to meet them. As I began to pray for God to use us to meet those needs, I realized we didn't have the resources. It was another revelation from Christ at work in me: *Rely on God's resources, not your own.*

Young people needed a safe place to drop in and hang out. They needed alternatives to illegal graffiti to express their creativity. Migrant young people needed classes in English as a second language. Students needed drug education, abstinence training, self-esteem coaching, and help in coping with bullying and abuse. There were young people in detention centers who needed visitors and positive influences. There were young people in trouble who needed someone they could trust.

The more I learned, the more I asked God to use us to meet those needs, and the more excited I became about the difference we could make in these young people's lives.

God used my naïveté and wide-eyed question asking,

and my inexperience with the financial constraints of such undertakings, to open doors of communication that I didn't know were seldom open between the culture and the church at the time. People will let you in if you are willing to serve. Businesses started offering supplies, paint, furniture, and even tradesmen to help us create our youth center. I walked into meetings relying on God and looking only for information and walked out with new friends who wanted to help us succeed.

I was discovering verses like James 4:2:

You do not have because you do not ask God.

It did not occur to me that the verse might not mean what it said. So I asked God for his provision for our youth center. I read, "The Lord is with you," so I just assumed that he was with me, and my growing confidence in him emboldened me as I went into each of my meetings. People started volunteering their help and services, which inspired more people to do the same, because they were all eager to see young people helped and at-risk young people guided in the right direction. I was seeing God answer prayers right before my eyes.

Christ in me was taking hold of my thinking and expanding his influence in my heart.

Every need, every idea, every potential resource went into the report I was preparing for Pastor John.

From what I'd researched so far and the resources we'd been offered, I figured we could open a drop-in center to get started. What a contrast to my old ways, when I wouldn't have dared to dream of beginning a new venture unless I'd been personally able to map out every detail. Seeing God provide such resources and so many people willing to help, I was catching on to the way he worked. God had a plan in place, and he was unfolding it before me. I was learning to put yet another principle to work: *Rely on God's ways and not your own.*

Did I mention that we were also given a building? That's right. We asked and were given the old police station as the new home of the Hills District Youth Service. It was as if, from day one, God wanted me to understand and believe that what he expected from me was a willing heart to place all that I had in his hands, expecting that he would provide the rest. And he did!

THE TRUE WORK OF THE BATON

One day, Pastor John said, "Chris, we've got to find a way to bring you on staff." There was nothing but a sixty-dollar-per-week provision for a janitor.

"Would you be willing to quit your job and accept a sixty-dollar-per-week stipend to come on full time as an associate director of the youth center?"

It was an absurd idea. I had just been offered a five-figure contract working for a shipping company.

"Yes, I'll do it!"

I'd been running, baton in hand, growing richer in my soul.

And this is when it dawned on me.

I'd thought the goal of the race was earning God's favor.

I'd thought the baton was good works.

I'd thought the race was about me trying hard enough to do enough good works for God, to earn his love.

But that wasn't it at all!

Since Pastor John had tossed me that pager—that baton—the carrying of that baton had been transforming me. As I'd seen God provide answers to prayer, I'd learned to rely on God's power rather than my own. My faith in him had grown. My trust in him had expanded. My love for him had deepened. Do you understand?

- The goal of the race *is not* to earn God's favor. *The goal is to become more like Christ.*
- The baton *is not* doing good works. *The baton is Christ at work in me and through me to the world.*
- Receiving the baton is not simply accepting a task. *Receiving the baton is inviting God to work in me and through me.*

- The race *is not* my lifelong efforts to earn God's love. *The race is becoming like Christ.*
- The exchange zone is not where I come for more works to do. *The exchange zone is the transformation zone.*

Two things are at work as Christ in us expands:

- One: Christ in us transforms us to be like him. This is called sanctification. Remember from Colossians, *"live a life worthy of the Lord, . . . growing in the knowledge of God."*
- Two: Christ in us transforms the world through us. He loves this world through meeting needs. This is what works are about.

When we carry the baton, *both* things are accomplished! The interplay of works and transformation to Christlikeness becomes an unstoppable, self-perpetuating cycle. The more we become like Christ, the more we love God, so the more we love people and the more works we want to do to help them.

Do you see why I want to spend my life eagerly running into the exchange zone for baton after baton after baton? I never want to stop! And once you experience the power of God working in and through you, I believe you won't want to stop either! Every baton brings us closer to Christlikeness. Every baton displays his love and power to the world. As long as we run, Christ in us is at work.

> *Being confident of this, that he who began a good work in you will carry it on to completion until the day of Christ Jesus.*
>
> Philippians 1:6

BECOMING WHOM YOU'RE RUNNING TOWARD

The Bible is full of ordinary people whom God called to his divine relay. Which of them, in their power, their resources, or their ways had what was required to do what God called them to do?

Not one.

Moses was told to lead his people from slavery, then was caught between Pharaoh's chariots and the Red Sea. Joshua was told to conquer the walled city of Jericho armed with nothing more than trumpets. Gideon was told to defeat the massive Midianite army after the Lord purposefully shrank his army from 32,000 men to only 300 armed with nothing more than trumpets, torches, and empty jars. Peter was beckoned by Jesus to get out of the boat and walk on water.[1]

Carrying the baton in our race is never about what *we* can accomplish *for* God. If he wanted, God could accomplish everything on his own without us. He could have slain Pharaoh's army and horses in midstep and melted the chariots in the blink of an eye. He could have brought the walls of Jericho down as Joshua and his men were sleeping. He could have turned the massive Midianite army to stone before Gideon's men blew a trumpet. He could have transformed the wild waves beneath Peter's feet to solid rock. God's goal in each of those cases was to do far more than accomplish a task—it was to build the faith of his people.

As you continue in your race, refuse to focus on what you are not, what you cannot do, and what you do not know. Rely on God's power. Rely on God's resources. Rely on God's ways.

I pray that out of his glorious riches he may strengthen you with power through his Spirit in your inner being, so that Christ may dwell in your hearts through faith. And I pray that you, being rooted and established in love, may have power, together with all the Lord's holy people, to grasp how wide and long and high and deep is the love of Christ, and to know this love that surpasses knowledge—that you may be filled to the measure of all the fullness of God.

THE MYSTERY REVEALED

*Now to him who is able to do immeasurably
more than all we ask or imagine, according to his
power that is at work within us, to him be glory
in the church and in Christ Jesus throughout all
generations, for ever and ever! Amen.*

Ephesians 3:16–21

⌒ SEVEN ⌒
THROW IT OFF

When you get to Greece, you will do whatever your cousin tells you to do," the witch doctor said.

And Favour, kneeling before the witch doctor, repeated, "When I get to Greece, I will do whatever my cousin tells me to do."

"You will not speak to strangers."

"I will not speak to strangers."

"You will not tell anyone who took you to Greece."

"I will not tell anyone who took me to Greece."

"And if you do, you will die or go mad."

Favour gasped. *Those* words she could not bring herself to repeat.

And why was she having to repeat *any* words a witch doctor prompted her to say?

"I was brought up by my dad and stepmother in

74

Nigeria," Favour said, "and they treated me very badly. They beat me all the time." When she was eighteen, her cousin invited her to come to Greece. "I accepted because I needed money to study to become a nurse. I have a passion to care for people and give them hope. I was excited!"

But then the cousin told her that before she left Nigeria, she would need to see a witch doctor. "I was so scared! When he asked me to say that I would die or go mad if I broke my oath, I refused. But then they told me that if I did not say the words, I would not leave the witch doctor's house alive, and I believed them. So I repeated his words—I said the oath. And then he made me say that if I even *told* anyone about the oath, I would die. I believed that it was true."

HELD CAPTIVE BY THE ENEMY

We have an enemy in this race. This enemy prowls about like a lion, seeking whom he may devour. If we run our race well, he has so much to lose!

He will plot and scheme to slow us down, to stop us in our tracks. We must not carry any additional weight into the race that the enemy could use against us. The writer to the Hebrews encourages us:

> *Let us throw off everything that hinders and the*
> *sin that so easily entangles. And let us run with*
> *perseverance the race marked out for us.*
>
> Hebrews 12:1

Favour's story is one of my favorites, because in her example we can all find the courage to throw off whatever hinders us in our own race.

FREEDOM FOR FAVOUR

Despite the frightening oath that Favour was forced to take before her cousin would bring her to Greece, Favour was excited to go. Her cousin had been like a sister. But soon after Favour arrived, her cousin had another woman physically beat Favour—for no apparent reason at all. After the beating, her cousin revealed what the promised job was to be: Favour would work as a prostitute. "I told her I could not do it. I could not sleep with men. But she told me that this was the only way to pay her back the money she used to bring me to Greece—60,000 euros.

"I saw no way out. I didn't know anyone and didn't want to die from breaking the oath. And I knew that if I didn't do what she wanted, she would beat me.

"Every day was like living in hell. Sometimes I had

to service forty or fifty men a day. There were times when I wanted to commit suicide. When I got home, my cousin would take all the money from me. 'Remember the oath,' she would say, 'or you will go mad and die.'"

Favour survived two years of this—two years of praying that God would get her out of her living hell—until one day, at the medical clinic where the prostitutes were required by Greek law to report to be checked for diseases, a woman who had been sitting in the waiting room approached her. It was Kalli, part of the staff at our A21 shelter in Greece.

Favour asked Kalli where she was from. When Kalli told her that she was from South Africa, Favour said quietly, "Speak English, then—the madam doesn't understand it." The madam from the brothel always accompanied the girls to the clinic.

The two women spoke in English, and every now and then one of them would say something silly, and they would laugh as if they were just chatting. But actually, Kalli was asking Favour for her story, and when she found out that Favour was a sex slave, Kalli asked why she didn't go to the police. "They told me that if I go to the police," Favour said, "they will tell their associates in Nigeria, who will kill my family."

The two women began to meet secretly before or after Favour's shift at the brothel. "Kalli spoke to me about Jesus for four months," Favour said. "Finally, I desired to accept Jesus because I believed that he is the only one who can save me from the pain of the life I lived. So one day, when I got home from the brothel, I prayed by myself on my bedroom floor to accept Jesus."

Not long after that night, the police, after months of investigation, conducted a raid on Favour's cousin's home and arrested everyone living there—her cousin, her cousin's boyfriend, and Favour. They were taken to the police station, and Kalli privately met Favour there.

Kalli brought Favour to the A21 safe house, where she met other girls who had been in the same situation. They gave her a room to sleep in and food to eat. She was witnessing the love of God through the love in action of the A21 staff.

When the date for the trial of her traffickers came up, Favour was so afraid of facing them again, particularly her cousin, that when she got to the courthouse, she was shaking. The trial lasted two days. Favour said, "When the lawyers called and told us that the traffickers had been sentenced to four years in jail, I jumped up and down for joy. A weight had been lifted off my shoulders. I could live again!"

That day, Favour realized that she belonged not to her sex traffickers but to Jesus. But there was more to becoming free, she discovered, than escaping the brothel. She'd suffered all her life. She'd spent years contending with nightmares and fears, shame and guilt, feelings of worthlessness and hopelessness.

She had to shed those hindrances that kept her entangled in the emotions and attitudes of her old life. And a huge part of that was learning to forgive.

"The ones I found it hardest to forgive were my father, because he drove me away from home; my stepmother, because she treated me badly; and my cousin, because she lied to me and made me sleep with men for money. Those things hurt me badly, and forgiving those three took me a very long time."

For her, as for us all, forgiveness was . . . complicated. But the same God who is accessible to you healed Favour's heart over time. As she grew to know God better, as she immersed herself in his Word, as she experienced the tender care of her A21 friends, Favour invited God to become bigger in her life than the injustices she'd suffered. And because she did, she was able to throw off those things that hindered her and step into the "exceedingly abundantly above" future (Ephesians 3:20 NKJV) that God had prepared for her before the foundations of the world.

That same hope exists for us all.

In Favour's case, casting aside that baggage made it possible for her to follow God's leading into a dream she had long held: "Today I am in nursing school, living independently in a rented house. A21 is still helping me with my living and school expenses. God has used them to restore my life and to help make my dreams come true. The time I spent with them has changed my life. They taught me how to forgive, how to make friends, how to love and care for others. All of my life is new."

CHOICES

Favour faced a choice: She could have surrendered to the temptation to harbor hate and resentment. Who would have more right to do that than Favour? But that was not the choice she made. If Favour, so young in her faith and so betrayed by life, can cast aside the entanglements that would hinder God's work in her life, you can do the same.

What are some of those things that hinder and entangle?

- Unforgiveness
- Bitterness
- Shame
- Rejection
- Offense
- Lust
- Greed
- Envy
- Deceit
- Insecurity
- Fear
- Doubt
- Indifference
- Apathy
- False belief systems

Do any of those things sound familiar? Does it sound like I took that list right from your own life?

I didn't. I took it from mine.

I was left in a hospital, unnamed, and unwanted—I was marginalized because of my ethnicity, gender, and socioeconomic background. I was also sexually abused as a child. But these things did not stop God from using me. He used me not in spite of my past but *because* of my past!

The past is set and can't be changed. But I *can* make choices today that will determine my future. And so can you. By putting God at the center of our lives, by dealing with the issues that hold us back, and by recognizing that the plans of God for our future are bigger than the pain and regret of our past, we are able to get up from wherever we are at this moment and move forward.

I am so grateful I reconciled my past in Christ and moved on to the future he has for me.

Cleaning out and renovating our internal world requires an ongoing, focused commitment. If I've made it sound as if throwing off these things was a one-time shot that, once accomplished, was never required again, let me correct that. We must learn and continually relearn to focus on *Christ in us* at work.

I don't know what your past is. I don't know what pains or sorrows or sins you carry. But I do know that God can turn all of it around and use your past to give someone else a future. That's what Jesus does.

FORGETTING WHAT IS BEHIND

We all have things we need to throw off. So take a moment right now. Ask yourself, "What do I need to throw off in order to run well?" The list could be endless. Perhaps you are carrying resentment or selfishness or pride that is hindering your witness at your job. What about unresolved anger that is hurting your relationships? Or a lack of confidence and a spirit of defeat that hinder your ability to make wise choices? Does deep-rooted anger continue to resurface in your marriage, causing you to say things you later regret? Does insecurity about your abilities or looks cause you to be judgmental and critical of others?

Are you tethered to destructive friends, favorite sins, unhealthy lifestyles, or negative habits? Are you too enamored with positive things such as financial gain, career success, or plentiful leisure time that hold you back from giving the time and energy to run the race God calls you to run?

Throw it off. Live free from your past mistakes, hurts, and misconceptions. "The old has gone, the new is here!" the apostle Paul said in 2 Corinthians 5:17. That applies to the refuse of your past—and to the hope for your future.

Old habits die hard. Breaking our comfortable, familiar patterns takes work. Hard work. But if we don't break from our past, we'll never run toward our new future.

Here is the simple truth: We cannot go where we are going without leaving where we have been. So ask yourself, "What must I leave behind in order to serve God with my whole life?" God is looking for runners who, like Paul, will say:

> *Whatever were gains to me I now consider loss for the sake of Christ. What is more, I consider everything a loss because of the surpassing worth of knowing Christ Jesus my Lord, for whose sake I have lost all things. I consider them garbage, that I may gain Christ.*
>
> Philippians 3:7–8

Imagine the freedom that will come when you are willing to lose that garbage for the surpassing greatness of becoming an unstoppable runner! Anticipate the joy of moving forward into the future he has for you! Toss away the garbage from your past and eliminate any way to go back. Make a defining decision of unhindered commitment to Jesus Christ and his cause, and step out in faith.

Do you want God to do something new in your life? Then stop doing the same old thing.

Do you want God to change your circumstances? Then be willing to change your life.

One thing I do: Forgetting what is behind and straining toward what is ahead, I press on toward the goal to win the prize for which God has called me heavenward in Christ Jesus.

Philippians 3:13–14

YOU CAN CHANGE THE FUTURE

Once you've thrown off what you should not be holding on to, you are free to grasp new batons.

When you are living for the race, you'll be running that race all week long, all month long, all year long, and all life long. You'll be intentionally and purposefully carrying your baton into the building where you work, into your interactions with your neighbors, into your community, your school, your grocery store, your bank, even your own kitchen.

Just consider the power of carrying your baton into those places rather than dragging along the ball and chain of hurts and resentments, sins and scars, and old priorities that are not God's priorities. Such freedom awaits you as you throw off those things that hinder you.

Are you ready to put an end to all that holds you back? Then do so. Put an end to it.

I have often thought of the story of Joseph—beloved by his father but betrayed and sold into slavery by his jealous brothers, betrayed by others and thrown into prison but rescued by God and raised to a position of prominence and power. *"You intended to harm me,"* he later told his brothers when God enabled him to use that position of power to help his whole tribe, *"but God intended it for good to accomplish what is now being done, the saving of many lives"* (Genesis 50:20).

Cut yourself free from all that hinders and cast it all away, so you can experience the truth of Psalm 40:1–3:

> *I waited patiently for the Lord;*
> *he turned to me and heard my cry.*
> *He lifted me out of the slimy pit,*
> *out of the mud and mire;*
> *he set my feet on a rock*
> *and gave me a firm place to stand.*
> *He put a new song in my mouth,*
> *a hymn of praise to our God.*
> *Many will see and fear the Lord*
> *and put their trust in him.*

∾ EIGHT ∾

MASTER THE
HANDOFF

I have always known one thing," Annie said. "I want to change the world. Careful what you ask for, right?"

Annie, a master of handing off batons to others in the race, is in fact changing the world, though not without cost. But she'll be the first to tell you that she wouldn't trade her journey for the world. When you learn to master the handoff, your race is not marred by sadness or regrets. When God determines that it is time to hand off a baton, it is only because we have taken it as far as we can, and he has something else for us to do.

Annie is a remarkable woman of God who joined Nick and me in the early days of our ministry. Before we had even officially started The A21 Campaign, it was Annie who led a research trip around the world and helped us build the infrastructure required to facilitate our work.

Remember Kristen? It was Annie who recommended that we offer her an internship and Annie who mentored her. She inspires, leads, trains, and mentors as she hands off batons. I sometimes suspect she needs an air traffic controller monitoring all the batons coming in for a landing.

"Over the years," Annie said, "my work has gone from building teams face-to-face in Nick and Chris's living room to helping build teams around the world. Only God could have multiplied our early efforts into such a dynamic and unstoppable movement. He has mobilized ten offices in nine countries, from volunteers cleaning toilets, to lawyers winning convictions against traffickers, to shelter moms, counselors, life-skills coaches, drivers, researchers, and prayer warriors.[1] He did it all one baton, one handoff at a time."

Annie has a bold willingness to release batons she loves for the sake of moving God's work forward in this world. When I first met her nearly twenty years ago, she'd recently relinquished a ministry she loved to follow God's call to move to Australia.

When it was time for Annie to move back to America to help us open our new office in California, she was hit with a surprise.

"The week before my move back to American soil,

a friend revealed that he was drawn to me and had been for some time. I thought the ocean would soon make it obvious that dating would not work. He kept texting, and eventually I found myself pulled into a long-distance relationship. I fought it. If there was one thing I knew about him it was this: he was called to build the church in Greece. Choosing him meant handing off batons I loved to carry."

Annie was torn between two countries—but she was loyal to only one kingdom, the kingdom of God. She was torn between two families—her beloved, close-knit biological family versus the family of God—but loyal to the one Father of both, almighty God.

"It took me two years," Annie said, "to make the decision to move to Greece. Thankfully, I'd be able to work out of our A21 office there, yet I knew that relocating would mean having to release batons so very close to my heart. I loved training our interns in our US office and overseeing the many programs I'd developed. I loved living in my homeland, the USA. There were many tears when I left, but after trying to fight loving this Greek man and trying to find any loophole that would allow me to walk away in good conscience, I *knew* I had to make this move."

And so she did. She opened her heart, opened her hand, and received the baton of engagement. Simultaneously, she developed a handoff plan for the long list of beloved ministry batons she'd been carrying. She didn't dread such change; she welcomed it, knowing that the future was in God's hands and the race was his. The handoff had always been her goal.

Annie offered God a heart of open expectation for the next leg of her own race. She had a new language to learn, a new culture to embrace, a new country to love. Annie had never been a wife. Now she'd be the wife of a pastor.

"Today, I am living in Thessaloniki, Greece," she said, "thrilled to be married to the man God led to me and still handing off batons locally and globally. I have no idea what batons are yet to come my way, but I know this: I still want to change the world, to advance the kingdom."

You, like Annie, will be called on to hand off your baton to others.

But what happens if you hold onto your favorite batons, never releasing them? Look at what, to me, is one of the saddest portions of Scripture. It is found in Judges 2.

A GENERATION WHO DID NOT KNOW GOD

Joshua was the man God chose to lead the children of Israel into the Promised Land. He was a mighty man of faith and an inspiring leader, but look what happened:

*The people served the Lord throughout the lifetime
of Joshua and of the elders who outlived him and
who had seen all the great things the Lord had
done for Israel.*

> *Joshua son of Nun, the servant of the Lord,
died at the age of a hundred and ten.... After
that whole generation had been gathered to their
ancestors, another generation grew up who knew
neither the Lord nor what he had done for Israel.*

Judges 2:7–8, 10

Joshua and his generation dropped the baton from
one generation to the next. By God's grace, they had
defeated the Amalekites,[2] crossed the Jordan River on
dry ground, seen the walls of Jericho come down, and
even seen the sun stand still. Yet after all these miracles,
the next generation—an *entire* generation—did not
know the Lord or the work he had done for Israel.

What happened? Where was the legacy of Joshua's
generation?

Someone somewhere dropped the baton of faith.

WHAT DO WE HAND OFF?

As the church, we are entrusted to pass the baton of
faith from one generation to the next.

Since our race is focused on Jesus and his work, we'd best turn to him to ensure we understand *his* priorities. What is at the heart of this "work" he wants to do in us and through us? Jesus told us in no uncertain terms. A teacher of the law asked him this question:

> *"Teacher, which is the greatest commandment in the Law?"*
>
> Matthew 22:36

Jesus's answer has come to be called the Greatest Commandment.

> *Jesus replied: "'Love the Lord your God with all your heart and with all your soul and with all your mind.' This is the first and greatest commandment. And the second is like it: 'Love your neighbor as yourself.'"*
>
> Matthew 22:37–39

Our top priority is to love God with everything we are and to love our neighbor. *Love is the work of Christ*— both in us and through us to the world. Learning to love God—so completely, so entirely that we do so with every fiber of our heart, soul, and mind—is a lifelong process. *Christ in us* has a lot of work to do! We are capable of loving God only because he first loved us.

After his resurrection, before he ascended to heaven, Jesus made a second crystal-clear statement about his greatest priorities. We know it as the Great Commission.

> *Go and make disciples of all nations, baptizing them in the name of the Father and of the Son and of the Holy Spirit, and teaching them to obey everything I have commanded you.*
> Matthew 28:19–20

The Great Commission is clearly the logical outgrowth of the Greatest Commandment. If we love God with all that we are, then we want to enjoy him and be with him and live in his presence forever. Right?

So likewise, if we love our neighbors as ourselves, we want them to know and enjoy that same thing; we want them to know God, enjoy him, and live in his incomparable presence all the days of their lives on earth and for all eternity. True?

Therefore, the more the Greatest Commandment grows in our lives, then the more the Great Commission grows in our lives.

Do you see the critical link here?

If we love, then we want to disciple. We cannot do the one without the other.

I want to propose a radical thought for you to consider.

I believe that *every* baton God gives us puts into practice one or both priorities of God. The work of Christ in us, his work in our own lives and through us to the world, fulfills either the Greatest Commandment (to love) or the Great Commission (to make disciples) or both.

MASTERING THE HANDOFF

A beautiful chain reaction began on the cross two thousand years ago. In order for that chain reaction to continue from you to countless others, everything hinges on your willingness and ability to make the handoff.

I've experienced the challenges of the handoff, and I've discovered that the following principles help ensure a seamless handoff.

GOODBYE TO BOTTLENECK AND HELLO TO MULTIPLICATION.

When you're maxed out on your capacity—overstressed and overworked—that could be a flashing alert that it's time to multiply your efforts through a handoff. Otherwise you become a bottleneck and hinder the growth that could happen.

Look for clues that you've hit your maximum capacity and welcome those clues as opportunities to make a handoff.

GOODBYE TO OWNERSHIP AND HELLO TO STEWARDSHIP.

Our ministry can be like our baby. When I was first handed the baton of fighting human trafficking, I thought, *I don't know how to do this!* But as we receive and run and truly *own* the baton we are given, we figure it out and get it running smoothly. How easy to slip into wrongly thinking that we now "own" that ministry. It's funny, but I've learned that when we say this, we can almost bank on a handoff coming soon. Why? Because we never own the work of God. We are simply stewards of it.

GOODBYE TO CONTROL AND HELLO TO CHANGE.

Once we've handed off a baton, it's going to look a little bit different. It may be improved—at which point you'll have to keep your ego in check. It may be dramatically changed—at which point you must remember it is God's ministry, not yours. Do you find yourself tempted to think, *I can do it better*? That's a great time to grow your teaching and coaching skills. If you train well, then that person can run while you accomplish new work, and that person will multiply many times over. They are supposed to be *like God*, not you!

GOODBYE TO INSECURITY AND HELLO TO HUMILITY.

Recognize when your identity has become too caught up in your role. This is as true in organizational handoffs as it is in family life and relationships. Your identity is in Christ, not in what you do. We must learn to celebrate that ministry goes on beyond us rather than secretly hope that it falters so that everyone will think we are irreplaceable. Beware of the enemy. Keep your eyes focused on Jesus. He is the hero, not you and not me.

GOODBYE TO THE PAST AND HELLO TO THE FUTURE.

Things in the ministry have grown so far beyond me that I do more vision-casting than setting up infrastructure. I now get to step back and empower others to do everything that I personally do not need to do. If you truly believe that what God has for you *next* is better than where you are now, and that what he has for the next person coming up is better for the race and for them, you will be eager for the next person to excel beyond what you did. It is never about me, me, me. It is all about God, God, God. It is God who prepares, who raises up, who anoints and appoints.

FROM ONE GENERATION
TO THE NEXT

The single most important place to run is into the lives of
the people God has placed in your circle—your children,
your spouse, your brother, your sister, your coworkers,
your friends, and your neighbors.

Are you a parent? Consider this:

> *These commandments that I give you today are to*
> *be on your hearts. Impress them on your children.*
> *Talk about them when you sit at home and when*
> *you walk along the road, when you lie down and*
> *when you get up.*
> Deuteronomy 6:6–7

Nick, the girls, and I take time every day that we
can to share with one another all the great things that
God is doing in our own lives and ministry. Even as
Nick and I nurture our marriage, we are handing off
trust and sacrificial love to each other while modeling
it for our girls. The media, educators, and politicians do
not have the responsibility to carry the baton of faith to
a generation—nor will they. It is our job.

Of course, carrying the baton to the next generation
is not only for parents. Every aspect of your life—every
decision you make and every action you take—serves

to either keep the relay moving or, conversely, to hinder the race.

No matter how fast-paced your life is, you can always find a way to turn the normal, inconsequential moments into eternal moments. Traveling with a coworker on business? What about a coffee break? Going shopping with a friend? Casually talk about a Bible verse that struck you or a life concern you've taken to God in prayer.

All that we do is an opportunity to either carry the baton of faith until we put it in the hands of the next generation or drop the baton. Short-term decisions will result in immediate gratification, but in order to fulfill our purpose, we must keep an eternal perspective. Faith is always only one generation from extinction.

IF NOT YOU, THEN WHO?

If we do not declare the greatness of our God working through the ages, then who will? This is our moment in history as the body of Christ. This is *your* moment as a member of the body of Christ. As you hand off one baton after another, never lose sight of God's cause. Will you run into the exchange zone and hand off the baton of faith for the next generation?

May you gain so much momentum while the baton is in your hand that you help catapult the next generation into all God has for them. May they run faster, harder, and greater than any generation before them. We run to his glory, for his glory, shining his glory so that others may see his glory.

> *One generation commends your works to another;*
> *they tell of your mighty acts.*
> *They speak of the glorious splendor of your majesty—*
> *and I will meditate on your wonderful works.*
> *They tell of the power of your awesome works—*
> *and I will proclaim your great deeds.*
> *They celebrate your abundant goodness*
> *and joyfully sing of your righteousness.*
>
> Psalm 145:4–7

NINE

FUELED BY PASSION

"Chris, my car is broken down, and I won't be able to do the 11:00 a.m. lecture on effective evangelism at the Bible college today. Can you please cover for me?"

Without thinking, I said yes to my friend John, not knowing that this unexpected baton was going to be a defining moment for my life.

I stepped into the classroom unprepared. Playing last-minute substitute wasn't a comfortable role for me. I have no recollection of what I taught that day.

A few weeks later, while at my gym for my 6:00 a.m. swim, I noticed that a young man who had been in the classroom on the day of my lecture was already swimming laps. We nodded and smiled, and I thought little of it until the next day and the next.

Before long, I learned that his name was Nick

Caine. He'd worked in the financial markets, he told me, until he had a revelation that his life was meant for more. One day, he ran into a former colleague who invited him to a church meeting, and instantly Nick responded to the message of the gospel. Overnight, he enrolled in Bible school.

Today when Nick tells this story, he simply says, "I fell in love with the teacher." Yep. He loved me before I loved him.

Fortunately, he didn't tell me that at the pool! I considered myself president of the Singles-Till-Rapture Club. I thought that by accepting the baton of ministry, I would never have the baton of marriage, and frankly, that suited me just fine.

Nick started showing up as a volunteer at our youth center. He said he figured that if I got to know him, I would not be able to resist him. I guess he was right, because before long I found myself hoping I would bump into him. He had a sharp mind, a keen wit, passionately loved Jesus and the church—and did I mention he was cute?

We transitioned from intense conversations about ministry while working side by side at the youth center to conversations over coffee, then picnics. I still don't know how that happened. Maybe it was the day he showed up with an invitation for a picnic at the park. "I didn't know what you like to eat," he explained as he opened his trunk, revealing four different types of bread, six different cheeses, ten different meats, and salads in case I was a vegetarian.

What kind of guy would even think like that?

I found myself besotted with him.

Passion is like that, isn't it? When new love invades your heart, the grass looks greener. The sky looks bluer. And the energy! Where does it come from?

As we drew closer, I began to realize that the brokenness of my past had built walls around my heart. Nick sensed my pain and worked with me through my healing process. He was patient and undeterred.

DRIVEN BY PASSION

When you are passionate about someone or something, you do not take no for an answer. You are unstoppable in your determination to find a way. Passion will enable you to do what you would never do if you didn't have it.

When Nick asked me to marry him, I was shocked. Was this part of my race? I'd believed I could accomplish far more for the gospel as a single woman.

One night, I was speaking at a youth rally of about a thousand kids. Before I stepped onto the stage I prayed, *Father, if I'm going to go further with this guy, I have to know that I'm going to do more for your kingdom married than I am single. I have to know. Do I keep dating this guy?*

I sensed God's response to me out of Deuteronomy 32:30, which says, *"How could one man chase a thousand, or two put ten thousand to flight?"*

Chris, God was saying to me, *you can choose whichever one you want. If you don't marry Nick, this is what you will have. You will have one thousand, like tonight. For your whole life wherever you go, I'll use you. But one will chase one thousand to flight. Two will put ten thousand to flight. So if you do marry him, you will have a tenfold impact for my kingdom.*

I called Nick and told him my conviction, and that I didn't see how I would be a traditional wife.

"Christine," he said, "what am I supposed to tell God on judgment day? Am I supposed to say, 'Lord, I'm sorry for all the millions of people who did not hear the gospel because I was too insecure to let Christine go out and evangelize? I'm sorry that I never let her go. And I'm sorry that all these people went to hell?'"

Nick wanted me to keep running the race. He simply wanted us to run together. He was so secure in himself and his relationship with God that having a wife in a leadership role in a national ministry was not a threat to him but an honor.

I thought, *Lord, I can marry that kind of man.*

And so I did. That is the power of passion!

Passion enlarged my heart. God did not give me

the baton of marriage to drop the baton of ministry; he gave me Nick to help carry the baton of ministry. God gave me the gift of the most determined, committed, selfless, unstoppable man I've ever met.

But Nick wasn't the first one to pursue me.

God passionately pursued me. When his love and grace captivated my heart, I wanted to run with God and run toward him. Thus began a lifetime love affair of responding to the love of God by pursuing the One who had pursued me.

His relentless pursuit of me was the starting gun for running my race, and passion for him fuels my continued focus on the finish line. For Nick and me alike, Christ in us is both the source of our passion and the sustainer of our passion.

When we aren't passionate about God and his purpose for our lives, the race becomes a "have to" instead of a "want to." The divine relay becomes little more than a series of good works and accomplishments for the purpose of earning God's love and approval.

But when we start our race knowing we are already deeply loved, valued, and accepted by God, then we are unstoppable as we carry our baton forward from a place of grace. We don't run to perform for or earn the approval of God. We run from the place of already being accepted by God.

KEEPING YOUR LOVE ALIVE

When you are fueled by the love and grace of God, every step of your run will be part of the adventure of your love affair with Jesus. But maintaining that passion is not something that happens automatically.

Passion, you see, is not a feeling. It's a decision. Decisions can be made and actions taken to consistently fuel our passion. Nick and I nurture our passion by making decisions. The same is true of our relationship with God, and yours too. When you know how much God loves you, you run your race from a place of deep security, fueled by this love.

I have found that by reminding myself of the following truths and intentionally taking these actions, I can remain consistent in my passion for God despite what is happening around me.

GOD PURCHASED ETERNAL LIFE FOR YOU WITH THE BLOOD OF HIS ONLY SON, SO KEEP YOUR LOVE ALIVE BY RUNNING YOUR RACE OUT OF JOY, NOT OBLIGATION.

Nothing demonstrates God's love for you more powerfully than the cross. *"You are not your own; you were bought at a price"* (1 Corinthians 6:19–20). Jesus wasn't forced to die for you. He chose the cross out of love for you. Jesus's passion for you took him to the cross—through the pain, through the humiliation, through the separation from God—and then to the resurrected life he lives to share with you. Now that is passion!

As you run, you express your love back to him. Run your race as a love gift, for the joy of blessing God. *"For the joy set before him he endured the cross, scorning its shame, and sat down at the right hand of the throne of God"* (Hebrews 12:2). For the joy of it, pour out your life for him.

GOD LOVED YOU BEFORE YOU LOVED HIM, SO KEEP YOUR LOVE ALIVE BY TELLING HIM YOU LOVE HIM . . . EVERY SINGLE DAY.

God created your inmost being. He knit you together in your mother's womb. He knows the number of hairs on your head. He delights in you and loves your company. He designed you with a purpose and has good plans for your future. There is nothing you can do to make him love you more or less. *"We love because he first loved us"* (1 John 4:19). Tell him you love him. Speak words of love to him every day.

GOD SPEAKS HIS LOVE INTO YOUR LIFE, SO READ HIS LOVE LETTER TO YOU—THE BIBLE—DAILY.

Nick told me that he loved me. He whispered it. He wrote it. He declared it over and over, and as he did, I drank it in like a thirsty sponge. God's love for you can do the same. Do you long to hear his voice declaring his love for you? There isn't a day that goes by that I don't talk to Nick or connect with him in some way, and I would be crazy to think that my relationship with God should be any different if I want to keep my passion alive. I don't know how else to say this other than to just say it: READ YOUR BIBLE. My prayer for you is that you may *"experience the love of Christ, though it is too great to understand fully. Then you will be made complete with all the fullness of life and power that comes from God"* (Ephesians 3:19 NLT).

GOD REJOICES OVER YOU WITH SINGING, SO KEEP YOUR LOVE ALIVE BY GIVING HIM YOUR THANKS AND PRAISE.

"He will take great delight in you; in his love he will no longer rebuke you, but will rejoice over you with singing" (Zephaniah 3:17). Respond by delighting him with words and music of praise and gratitude. I believe that music is an untapped treasure chest that can carry the heart of God, shift the atmosphere of a room, and help change our perspective in the midst of our circumstances. The Bible says to *"enter his gates with thanksgiving and his courts with praise"* (Psalm 100:4). When you find it difficult to connect with God or stir your passion for him, start by thanking him for all he has done and then find a worship song to sing as a declaration of his promise in the midst of your current situation.

GOD HEALS YOUR PAIN AND BRINGS HEALING INTO YOUR LIFE, SO DISPLAY YOUR LOVE TO HIM BY BRINGING HEALING TO OTHERS.

Nick walked alongside me as I slowly learned to move beyond my past. You can love God back by looking for opportunities to be the hands and feet of Jesus, seeking to ease the pain of the broken people in this world. *"Dear children, let us not love with words or speech but with actions and in truth"* (1 John 3:18).

Here is one other idea. Have you ever written out the story of God's relentless pursuit of you? Try it. As I was composing this chapter and wrote out how Nick won my love, I felt compelled to go running to him to tell him all over again how grateful I am that he never gave up. Remembering our story re-stirred my passion.

THE WIDE-OPEN, EXPANSIVE LIFE

Did you know that the definition for *passion* is "an intense desire or enthusiasm for something"?[1] The word *enthusiasm* comes from two Greek words: *en* meaning "in or within," and *theos* meaning "God."

Yes! Passion means "in God." Sound familiar? *Christ in us! Christ in you!*

Christ in you means that you alone do not keep your God-passion alive. Have you ever tried to manufacture passion where it doesn't exist? But passion for the purposes of God is not something we manufacture within us under our own power. It is *supernatural.*

So open your life to the continual infilling of the Holy Spirit. Do you remember what Jesus told the disciples about the coming of the Holy Spirit after the resurrection, just before he ascended into heaven? *"I am going to send you what my Father has promised; but stay in the city until you have been clothed with power from on high"* (Luke 24:49).

That promised gift was the Holy Spirit, and it is the Spirit who *clothes us with the power from on high.* His passion fills us as he comforts us, teaches us, empowers us, counsels us, convicts us, and intercedes for us. So open up wide.

> *Dear, dear Corinthians, I can't tell you how much I long for you to enter this wide-open, spacious life. We didn't fence you in. The smallness you feel comes from within you. Your lives aren't small, but you're living them in a small way. I'm speaking as plainly as I can and with great affection. Open up your lives. Live openly and expansively!*
> 2 Corinthians 6:11–13 MSG

The wide-open life is about waking up every morning and knowing that *you were born for this day.* When I look into the eyes of my husband and children, when I see lives transformed through ministry and love, when I see God multiply what we offer him and make our "not enough" into more than enough, I taste this wide-open, expansive kind of life, and my passion to keep running the race grows.

What is it that drives Olympic athletes to get up early, push through pain, set aside distractions—for *years*? Passion.

What keeps Kalli and all the rest of our A21 staff at locations around the world going day after day, year after year? Passion.

What keeps Katja and Favour from descending into bitterness and instead moving toward recovery and forgiveness? Passion.

What kept the early Christians hard at work spreading the gospel, even though they saw their fellow believers imprisoned and tortured? Passion.

Passion drives the human heart to persevere through hardship when nothing else will keep us going.

Jesus's life on this earth was the ultimate picture of the passionate life. He embraced children, delighted in doing the will of the Father, healed the sick, loved the lost, helped the marginalized, dined with friends and neighbors, and gave his all to run his race.

May the same be true for you.

RUN THE RACE!

I am convinced that neither death nor life, neither angels nor demons, neither the present nor the future, nor any powers, neither height nor depth, nor anything else in all creation, will be able to separate us from the love of God that is in Christ Jesus our Lord.

Romans 8:38–39

ೕ෧ TEN ೕ෧
THE MAKING OF A CHAMPION

Phil had received a text message the day before from the church office, asking him to meet with Nick. They'd never met before, but others had recommended Phil to Nick for a position at A21. As Nick shared staggering statistics and played heart-wrenching videos of trafficked women recounting their stories, Phil couldn't fathom why Nick had called him here to tell him such things. And then—the shocker. Nick wanted Phil to move to Greece and accept the position as head of the A21 efforts.

"Nick," Phil protested, "I've never been to Greece. I don't even speak Greek. I've never even heard of human trafficking before today. You don't even know me! Why me?"

Why me, indeed. Throughout the history of the divine relay, God has surprised people with illogical batons.

"All the way home and all that night my soul was screaming at God, 'What are you doing, Lord? This is not part of my plan,'" Phil said. "But somehow I knew this was God's leading. I'd been praying for months, *Lord, break my heart for what breaks yours. Not my will but yours be done with my life. I will go wherever you send me.* It had been easy to pray that way when I was certain that God's plans aligned with my own."

Phil accepted that baton. Did he feel ready? No. Did he feel qualified? No. "I didn't have adequate education for the job. I didn't know how to work with politicians and law enforcement, especially in a foreign land and foreign language. I'm not a counselor or psychologist or educator."

Phil knew that it was God who qualifies his runners, not man. "Suddenly, I realized God had been preparing me for this new direction. This was just crazy enough to be God!"

Phil embraced his place, willing to be uprooted from his comfort zone and transplanted into a foreign culture to do a job for which he had no training or experience.

He went from his first conversation with Nick in May to a research trip to Cambodia in June, where he saw, firsthand, victims in a shelter there. He was struck by the indisputable evidence that God had just placed him on the front lines of the battleground described in Ephesians.

> *Our struggle is not against flesh and blood, but against the rulers, against the authorities, against the powers of this dark world and against the spiritual forces of evil in the heavenly realms.*
>
> Ephesians 6:12

Phil had been called to fight.

In July, he landed in Greece to set up the A21 office, and within a month of receiving approval to operate a transition home, they received the first victim into care.

From the start, the enemy attacked him with thoughts of fear and inadequacy. He and our new team invaded the enemy's territory but were met with corruption and the insidious presence and power of the traffickers. For the first time in his life, Phil experienced the fear of being in real physical danger.

At night the screams of the women in their care awakening from nightmares pierced the quiet. The severity of their physical wounds sickened the team. The threat of hopelessness and despair drove them to their knees.

The words of Romans 8 came alive as never before.

What, then, shall we say in response to these things? If God is for us, who can be against us?... Who shall separate us from the love of Christ? Shall trouble or hardship or persecution or famine or nakedness or danger or sword?... No, in all these things we are more than conquerors through him who loved us.

Romans 8:31, 35, 37

WE ARE AT WAR

We are in a spiritual battle. The enemy does not want us to fulfill our destiny.

I won't sugarcoat it. Trials and storms will come to you. Obstacles will rise up. Challenges will multiply. There is always a fight in the exchange zone.

Why? Because the enemy has so much to lose. If he can persuade us to drop our batons, to stop running, imagine all the future handoffs and releases he would prevent.

God's divine relay threatens the enemy's territory, and he will not go down without a fight. Just read of his insidious attempts to tempt Jesus at the onset of his ministry[1] and of his work in Judas.[2] If he is bold enough to try to take on the Son of God, he won't hesitate to do his best to thwart us.

But here is the spectacular truth:

Greater is He who is in you than he who is in the world.

1 John 4:4 NASB

Jesus overcame the Evil One. God uses the enemy's tactics against him. What the enemy intends for evil, God uses for good. Yes, Satan used Judas to betray the Lord, but God intended for Jesus to stand trial and be condemned to death. Yes, Satan used the scheming of Jesus's enemies to have him crucified but, in so doing, Satan fulfilled God's plan for securing eternal life for all who believe in Jesus. Satan loses! God wins!

So what happens when the enemy attacks a runner in the divine relay? Do we allow these attacks, trials, and storms to stop us? No! God uses every single trial to our benefit, for our good.

Phil wasn't stopped by the enemy's attacks. He led our team in setting up a stellar safe house, then a legal office, then an anonymous tip line that opened the floodgates to reach more victims and gather more intelligence to win more court battles. The US State Department, in its 2012 Trafficking in Persons Report, named Phil as a hero, one of the ten most influential people in fighting trafficking, and Secretary of State Hillary Clinton personally presented him an award.[3]

Do you see how God uses obstacles to make us stronger when we refuse to stop running our race? God is building champions.

CHAMPIONS FIND GOD'S STRENGTH IN THEIR OWN WEAKNESS

It would be so much more comfortable if God would keep us in our "strength zone," wouldn't it? But God keeps thrusting us into our "weakness zone" because it is only in our weakness that he is made strong.

> *[Jesus] said to me, "My grace is sufficient for you, for my power is made perfect in weakness." Therefore I will boast all the more gladly about my weaknesses, so that Christ's power may rest on me. That is why, for Christ's sake, I delight in weaknesses, in insults, in hardships, in persecutions, in difficulties. For when I am weak, then I am strong.*
>
> 2 Corinthians 12:9–10

God is never limited by our limitations. Whenever he calls us to step out of our comfort zone and into the exchange zone, it is because he wants to do something in and through our lives.

Now, here is the critical question: How do we increase our willingness to trust in God's strength when our own weakness is so glaring that it captures all our focus? Let's turn to Peter's championship training.

TRAINED TO BE A CHAMPION

The disciples were getting nowhere. When they'd pushed off from shore just a few hours before, the water had been calm and the boat seemed to offer what they needed most—rest and solitude.

They'd just learned that John the Baptist had been executed. Jesus had led the disciples to withdraw to a quiet place to rest. But the locals—about five thousand men plus women and children—had discovered Jesus's location and soon swarmed them. Jesus miraculously fed everyone in the crowd with no more than five loaves and two fish. When that miracle was complete, Jesus told his disciples to "immediately" get into the boat and go to Capernaum on the other side of the lake while Jesus stayed behind to dismiss the crowd and then go off by himself to pray.

Let's focus in on Peter.

Peter was no novice in witnessing miracles.

Straining against the oars with every muscle,

Peter must have longed to have Jesus there in the boat with him. *If only the Lord were here*, he must have thought, *he would calm this windstorm before our eyes, like he did before.*

And then they saw him.

Let's pick up the story in Matthew 14:25–29.

Shortly before dawn Jesus went out to them, walking on the lake. When the disciples saw him walking on the lake, they were terrified. "It's a ghost," they said, and cried out in fear.

But Jesus immediately said to them: "Take courage! It is I. Don't be afraid."

"Lord, if it's you," Peter replied, "tell me to come to you on the water."

"Come," he said.

Then Peter got down out of the boat, walked on the water and came toward Jesus.

I love it! That's Peter. He was all in.

But when he saw the wind, he was afraid and, beginning to sink, cried out, "Lord, save me!"

Immediately Jesus reached out his hand and caught him. "You of little faith," he said, "why did you doubt?"

Matthew 14:30–31

Why *did* he doubt? Yesterday's miracles didn't yet outweigh his fear of today's dangers.

Can you relate? I believe we all can.

The danger of drowning was real. In a surge of ecstatic faith, he'd climbed out of the boat with his eyes fixed on Jesus, when it suddenly occurred to him that there was nothing under his feet but water.

And this is exactly why we *need* storms and trials in our lives if our faith is to grow.

UNTESTED FAITH IS FRAGILE

It's no coincidence that the windstorm "just happened" to occur on the heels of the miracle of the loaves and fish. Jesus is omniscient. He *chose* to be on land, a distance from his disciples, when the storm hit. And he *chose* his words carefully when he said to Peter, "You of little faith, why did you doubt?"

Jesus used Peter's moment of weakness as a teaching moment.

In Mark 6:51–52, a parallel rendering of the Matthew 14 account, we catch on to what Jesus was showing them in the middle of that storm.

> *Then he climbed into the boat with them,*
> *and the wind died down. They were completely*

amazed, for they had not understood about the loaves; their hearts were hardened.

They had not understood about the loaves. They had not grasped how that act had revealed the deity of Jesus—his identity as being one with God, and thus his omnipotent power over the physical world.

A few hours of fear must have softened those hardened hearts, because when Jesus came strolling along walking on top of the water, they got it.

And when [Peter and Jesus] climbed into the boat, the wind died down. Then those who were in the boat worshiped him, saying, "Truly you are the Son of God."
                                        Matthew 14:32–33

The storm had done its work!

TRIALS ARE THE ULTIMATE STRENGTH-TRAINING EXERCISE

Consider it pure joy, my brothers and sisters, whenever you face trials of many kinds, because you know that the testing of your faith produces perseverance. Let perseverance finish its work so

*that you may be mature and complete, not lacking
anything.*

James 1:2–4

The powerful message of this verse is clear—bad
news can be faced with great hope. Whether your trials
came as a result of your own brokenness or poor choices,
or because of the choices of someone else, or by an act
of nature such as a flood or an earthquake or a tornado,
or as a consequence of living in a fallen world, you have
reason, even while grieving and hurting, to be joyful.

Why?

Because trials test your faith.

Is it bad news when your weaknesses are revealed?
No! Better to have them revealed so we can acknowledge them and, with God's work inside us, see our
weakness rooted out.

But notice this in the James 1 verses: It is not God's
work alone.

God gives us two commands: *consider* and *let*. We
are to "consider it" pure joy. This requires us to make
a deliberate decision about how we view the trial. We
must "let" perseverance do its work by working with
God, not against him, in the face of our trials.

We, like Peter and Phil, have choices to make in
the face of life's trials. Peter reached for Jesus. He could
have sunk to his armpits and then, spitting mad, swum

back to the side of the boat, cursing Jesus for allowing him to sink. But he didn't. He cried out to Jesus, and Jesus reached for him. Phil could have decided he'd made a huge mistake and flown home to Denmark. But he didn't. He reached for God's strength and carried on in Greece. And do you know what happened next?

More tests. More trials. Obstacles. Hurdles. Of course! Phil was in championship training—and he still is. What else would we expect?

YOUR WALK-ON-WATER MOMENTS

Champions understand that God uses every trial to build our strength and endurance. This is why Jesus, knowing that within hours he would be arrested, flogged, paraded through the streets, and crucified, said the following words to us:

> *"All this I have told you so that you will not fall away. They will put you out of the synagogue; in fact, the time is coming when anyone who kills you will think they are offering a service to God. They will do such things because they have not known the Father or me. I have told you this, so that when their time comes you will remember that I warned you about them. . . . I have told you these things, so*

*that in me you may have peace. In this world you
will have trouble. But take heart! I have overcome
the world."*

John 16:1–4, 33

Do you hear him? Take heart! Be of good cheer!
Consider it all joy! Such times are when you will experience firsthand that greater is he who is in us than he
who is in the world.

Between the disciples and Jesus that windy night,
there was darkness, danger, and distance. Ever been
there? Your storm is raging "here" and Jesus seems to
be over "there." Jesus knows when you are in trouble,
when you have had enough, when you need strength
and courage. He knows when to calm the storm and
when to ride it out with you.

Climb out of that boat with your eyes fixed on
Jesus. And if you falter, cry out to him, reach out to
him, knowing he will catch you and climb into your
boat. He will calm the storm. Then he will step into
your weakness with his strength.

With this confidence, we can say, with Peter,

*In all this you greatly rejoice, though now for a little
while you may have had to suffer grief in all kinds
of trials. These have come so that the proven genu-
ineness of your faith—of greater worth than gold,*

which perishes even though refined by fire—may result in praise, glory and honor when Jesus Christ is revealed. Though you have not seen him, you love him; and even though you do not see him now, you believe in him and are filled with an inexpressible and glorious joy, for you are receiving the end result of your faith, the salvation of your souls.

1 Peter 1:6–9

ELEVEN

OUTRUNNING THE PASSION-SLAYERS

What do you see?" my professor asked as he projected a picture of a small black dot in the middle of a very big white screen. I was sitting in Psychology 101 during my years at Sydney University.

We all responded immediately: "A black dot."

I was excited, thinking, *If all of the questions are as easy as this one, this course is going to be easy!*

The prof asked again, "What do you see?"

We repeated even more loudly: "A black dot!"

Again he paused . . . and then asked the same question a third time.

Now he had my attention. And when still, on the third try, none of us provided the correct answer, he explained. "You were all so focused on the little black dot in the center of the screen that none of you noticed the dominant image on the screen: the large white space covering the screen top to bottom, left to right."

There was far more white space than black dot. There is *always* much more white space than there is space covered by little black dots—we simply need to recognize and focus on it.

The black dots of our lives—the trials, challenges, disappointments, obstacles, and hurdles we face as we run—will naturally draw and consume our attention. But Jesus is the "white space" of God's power at work in the universe, and the trials we face are but a tiny speck, a black dot, in comparison.

Phil experienced the truth of this. He could have focused on the black dots—the painful circumstances our team encountered, the fear of danger and of team members' inadequacies and personal failures, the discouragement of unmet expectations, relational strife, weariness, hopelessness, and the power of the enemy's opposition. All of those trials could have slain the passion that drove him and our team forward in their race.

But he and our team kept their eyes fixed on Jesus, the author of their faith and the one who would carry it to completion. They are champions in the making and are learning on the run to focus on that which is far bigger than those black dots—the white space of God at work.

It's not easy to go the distance, is it? There are casualties in this race. The battles can be fiercer, the mountains higher, the rivers wider, and the terrain rockier than you anticipated. The goals set before you will seem another inch away no matter how close you get. I told you I wouldn't sugarcoat it!

As we put our championship training to work, the enemy will do his best to drain our passion and wear us down to the point that we drop out of the race. The enemy who kills our passion steals the fuel that keeps us running.

THE PASSION-SLAYERS

The enemy works to draw our focus to the black dots of our lives and sow discontentment. I call these tactics the passion-slayers. My list is by no means exhaustive. But I've found that believers who've learned to conquer these tactics are well-equipped to handle just about anything the enemy can throw at them. Here's my list:

- Negative circumstances
- Fear
- Failure
- Unmet expectations
- Relational strife
- Weariness
- Opposition
- Hopelessness

Let's examine each of these passion-slayers and retrain ourselves to focus not on the black dots but on the vast white space of God's power at work.

NEGATIVE CIRCUMSTANCES: SEE THE INVISIBLE WORK OF GOD IN YOUR VISIBLE CIRCUMSTANCES.

What events and situations in your life have threatened to derail you? Whatever the circumstances may be, it's time to do what Paul says in 2 Corinthians 4:18: *"We fix our eyes not on what is seen, but on what is unseen, since what is seen is temporary, but what is unseen is eternal."*

Easy for you to say, you might be thinking. *You don't know what's going on in my life*. That's true, I don't—and I don't mean to in any way belittle the giants you may be facing. But I *do* know—and I want you to know—that God is bigger than any circumstances, no matter how daunting. Problems that seem overwhelming, that threaten to deplete your passion, can be made small in the light of God's greatness.

FEAR: SEE TRUST GROW WHERE FEAR REIGNED.

Fear surged through Phil when he stood face-to-face with the first victim who came into the care of the A21 shelter in Greece. He said, "Until then, I had read about victims, I had even witnessed them first-hand in Cambodia. But now I was standing there face-to-face with a broken woman. Her life was now my responsibility, and I felt so out of my boat. I felt such a heavy burden of responsibility, and I prayed, *Lord, I'm not prepared. How can I possibly be ready for this? What if I fail her?*"

Do you hear the whispers of the enemy? What if, what if, what if? It's important to recognize that voice so that you know a trial when you face one. Instead, listen to God's voice: *"For God has not given us a spirit of fear, but of power and of love and of a sound mind"* (2 Timothy 1:7 NKJV). The moment you taste fear, focus on the good news that you've just seen the territory where your faith is about to grow. When you learn to see areas of fear as places where trust is about to grow, fear gives way to courage.

FAILURE: SEE THE BUILDING OF YOUR CHARACTER THROUGH FAILURE.

Failing at something does not make you a failure. The race does not end when you fail; the race ends for you when you stop getting back up. Proverbs 24:16 tells us, *"For though the righteous fall seven times, they rise again."* The key is refusing to quit. Do not stop. Never. Ever.

Remember, it is not so much about what we accomplish for God, but that we are becoming like him. Failure, when offered to him, builds our humility and our reliance on him.

All of us have dropped one or several of the batons entrusted to us. But the good news is, it is never too late to pick up the baton where you are and once again run your race. Jesus has redeemed our lives so that we can all have forgiveness for our past, a fresh start today, and a hope for the future.

UNMET EXPECTATIONS: SEE GREAT EXPECTATIONS RATHER THAN UNMET EXPECTATIONS.

Phil arrived in Greece expecting to set captives free.

"That first year we went in expecting that all we had to do was open a home and we'd be flooded with women wanting help," Phil said. "However, when 99 percent of victims are never rescued, that means very few come out on their own accord, and even fewer come into care facilities. The enemy kept these women imprisoned as much by fear as by locked doors."

God, Phil prayed, *we need to get creative with new approaches to reach those we're here to help*. God answered. Phil explained, "We tried to put ourselves in the position of a trafficked victim. Where did she go? What did she see? Who would she interact with? How could we find ways to infiltrate her world and come alongside her?" Those questions generated a huge list of people our team had not expected to need to network with.

Phil's story illustrates exactly what we've been

discussing. Every one of the team's unmet expectations pushed them to expand their reach. So *Christ in us* was touching the lives of all the people the team networked with. This is the mystery at work.

This is the great race you are running in! So if you find yourself struggling with unmet expectations, cast them aside and keep running with great expectations to discover what God had in mind all along.

RELATIONAL STRIFE: SEE THE OPPORTUNITY FOR HARMONY RATHER THAN STRIFE.

As long as you are working with human beings, you will contend with grumblers or be in danger of becoming one. Misunderstandings will occur. Egos will flare. Selfish ambition will rear its head.

I have great news for you: Every time strife hits, you are being handed a beautiful opportunity to love like Jesus. God's Word spells out the guidelines. *"Make every effort to live in peace with everyone and to be holy; without holiness no one will see the Lord. See to it that no one falls short of the grace of God and that no bitter root grows up to cause trouble and defile many"* (Hebrews 12:14–15).

Live at peace with others, with no bitterness, so that others may see God at work in you. Love one another. Whenever strife begins, thank God for the opportunity to see the power of his love in action, then commit to addressing it and resolving it in love.

WEARINESS: SEE GOD'S REST IN
THE FACE OF WEARINESS.

In Matthew 11:28, Jesus beckons us, *"Come to me, all you who are weary and burdened, and I will give you rest."* When you are weary in body, mind, or soul, you must have rest, and doing so requires that you examine the reasons for your tiredness. Are you getting the sleep you need? Are you taking a Sabbath? Even the Son of God rested, so surely you must, too.

Sometimes we are weary because we don't know how to say no. Are there handoffs you've been reluctant to make? Are there burdens hindering you that you must throw off? Relinquish what is not yours to carry. Galatians 6:9 says, *"Let us not become weary in doing good, for at the proper time we will reap a harvest if we do not give up."* We cannot twist God's arm or make something happen in our own timing or strength. Our due dates are often different from God's appointed times. Stay faithful, trust God, and get some rest!

OPPOSITION: SEE GOD USE OPPOSITION
TO ACHIEVE HIS GOALS.

Phil at first felt intimidated by the evil he saw at work behind human trafficking. He thought he'd understood evil before, but as he looked into the eyes of those trafficked women, as he saw the physical and emotional scars, he knew he was standing face-to-face with an evil more twisted, more powerful, and more dangerous than he'd ever known.

But Phil and our team kept their eyes and their prayers focused on our omnipotent God. Phil refers to one particular trial against a major trafficker as "a real nail-biter," but the team appealed to believing friends on several continents to pray for victory. Phil reports, "The trafficker was sentenced to fifteen years in jail and a fine of 108,000 euros! This was a landmark case and the first of its kind in A21 history. But not the last. The opposition may have been great, but our God was greater."

HOPELESSNESS: SEE GOD'S WAY WHEN WE SEE NO WAY.

Hopelessness occurs when we no longer see any way forward. When all we can see is the black dot. If ever you find yourself there, be aware that you've lost sight of God's great white expanse. So step back. Refocus. Acknowledge that God has a way when you see no way. Everything we see that appears to be a giant, a road-block, the end, is but a tiny dot on the infinite white space of God's work in the universe!

Our hope is in Jesus, who is at the end of the race. Reach toward that hope. Focus on what it takes to finish and win. Because this race is the Lord's, and it's not over yet. God wins! As his runner, as long as you persevere, you win. Every day pray, *Lord, even if I cannot see you, I hope in you and trust you.* Hebrews 6:19–20 says, *"We have this hope as an anchor for the soul, firm and secure. It enters the inner sanctuary behind the curtain, where our forerunner, Jesus, has entered on our behalf."*

At times I have felt inadequate, unable, and unqualified. Yet these limitations have not stopped me from stepping into God's purposes for my life, because by choosing to grasp each baton God has given me, I have ultimately learned that it is not about my UN—it is about the ONE.

THE SECRET OF CONTENTMENT

God's Word provides us with a powerful secret that will enable us to outrun the passion-slayers. We can learn to be content in the midst of our trials.

The apostle Paul must have been a master of true contentment.

> *I have learned to be content whatever the circumstances. I know what it is to be in need, and I know what it is to have plenty. I have learned the secret of being content in any and every situation, whether well fed or hungry, whether living in plenty or in want.*
>
> **Philippians 4:11–12**

Notice that contentment didn't come naturally to Paul. It doesn't come naturally to any of us. Paul said, "I have *learned* to be content." He wrote not while vacationing on a Greek island resort but while sitting in a prison, being persecuted for his faith.

True contentment has nothing to do with our external circumstances but rather with our internal dependence on Christ and our confidence in the work he is doing. He gives us strength to do whatever we need to do and be whatever we need to be in the moment. Contentment, then, is found in Christ alone—in the presence of Jesus, not in the absence of difficulties.

This means that when discontentment creeps into our thinking, it is a red flag that we've taken our focus off Jesus and set it on the black dots of our circumstances. When that happens, do an instant course correction. Choose to see that *Christ in you* is at work. In fact, he can use every one of those black dots to take his work in you one step further. He can use them to make you stronger, wiser, faster—to shape you into the champion runner who will one day cross the finish line.

WE PRESS ON FOR THE PRIZE

Once we've discovered the secret of seeing those potential passion-slayers as nothing more than God's opportunity to defeat the enemy and complete his good work, then we are compelled to run all the harder.

No promise is too hard for God to keep.

No prayer is too hard for God to answer.

No problem is too hard for God to solve.

No person is too hard for God to save.

No mountain is too big for God to move.

No need is too great for God to meet.

There is nothing our God cannot do!

"No weapon forged against you will prevail,
and you will refute every tongue that accuses you.
This is the heritage of the servants of the Lord,
and this is their vindication from me,"
declares the Lord.

Isaiah 54:17

TWELVE

THE WINNER'S CIRCLE

Nick and I stood in the breathtaking Cologne Cathedral, the largest Gothic church in northern Europe.

I am one of those people who love to read the story behind monuments, so Nick went to grab an espresso while I satisfied my historical curiosity. I read that construction started in 1248 and took until 1880 to complete. Nothing great is built overnight. This magnificent cathedral was bigger than one generation.

We are part of something eternal, not merely temporal. We will run our race but will not see the finish line this side of eternity. We must run our race with conviction, mindful of that truth. And when the time comes, we must hand the baton to the next generation and take our seat with the cloud of witnesses to cheer them on.

The plans God has for us are so big that it will take

you and the generations that follow to comprehend and complete his work.

> *But the plans of the Lord stand firm forever,*
> *the purposes of his heart through all generations.*
> Psalm 33:11

WHAT LEGACY WILL WE LEAVE BEHIND?

Some legacies are filled with faith, forgiveness, hope, love, compassion, and generosity. Others contain things like anger, greed, racism, bitterness, and rejection. Many legacies contain a little of both. The question is not *if* we will leave a legacy, but rather *what* our legacy will be.

I believe the quality of our legacy is directly determined by how we run our race. When we choose to live a life that extends beyond ourselves and beyond today, we are showing coming generations that there is Someone big and grand who is worth living our life for and giving our life for.

Jesus said in Matthew 16:18, *"I will build my church, and the gates of Hades will not overcome it."* The kingdom of God is always advancing, showing the world that the church Jesus is building is magnificent and powerful, and neither the power of hell nor the schemes of humankind shall prevail against it. Jesus cares infinitely for the church. He gave his life for it.

This is our time in history to arise. As we run our leg of the race, we must always remember that *Christ in us*, who is working in and through us, is even greater *beyond* us, for he has been, is, and shall continue to be working through the ages.

Jesus's legacy of self-sacrifice is the richest, most remarkable, and startling legacy in the history of our planet:

> *Have the same mindset as Christ Jesus:*
> *Who, being in very nature God,*
> *did not consider equality with God something*
> *to be used to his own advantage;*
> *rather, he made himself nothing*
> *by taking the very nature of a servant,*
> *being made in human likeness.*
> Philippians 2:5–7

Once here, he embodied the love and mercy of God, teaching, healing, and working mighty miracles as he purposefully pursued his greatest legacy of all—the reason he came to this earth. As that time approached, he prepared his disciples, and when he knew they were prepared enough (though they didn't seem ready by human standards), he led them, of all places, to a garden. He was almost to the finish line.

THE FINISH LINE

When athletes compete, they picture their prize, the winner's cup, awarded in the circle of champions.

Often when new believers accept Christ, they begin with the focus that the Christian life is all about me, me, me—God saving me from hell, God solving my problems, God and me connecting in personal relationship. All good things, of course, but our earliest steps of faith are merely baby steps. Then we begin to grow in the knowledge of God, and for many, maybe for you, this is the point at which we realize there is a race to be run.

Reach. Receive. Release. Repeat. We embrace our place. We catch the rhythm. Life hits us, challenges hit us, we start doing the hard kingdom work and hit resistance, temptation, roadblocks, and persecution. Handoff after handoff, we carry Christ in us as he transforms us from the inside out and transforms our world through us. Eventually, we realize we aren't running against the other runners. We are a team, fueled by passion, all straining in sync against an enemy determined to stop us.

The enemy does not want us to reach the winner's circle. But we push through.

We picture name-engraved trophies, jeweled crowns, and revelry and celebration. And yes, that does await us, but it is still far off. There is more we don't quite grasp.

NEVERTHELESS

And He was withdrawn from them about a stone's throw, and He knelt down and prayed, saying, "Father, if it is Your will, take this cup away from Me; nevertheless not My will, but Yours, be done."
Luke 22:41–42 NKJV

Do you see it? Do you see the Winner's Cup? We've drunk from it since we first became believers, the blood of Jesus willingly poured out for us. But until now, we've never grasped that this is *our* Winner's Cup as well.

The Winner's Cup is SACRIFICIAL LOVE. When Jesus surrendered, he knew what was coming. The agony. The cost. The sacrifice. He knew the whip would tear the flesh on his back, that the thorns would pierce his brow. He knew that not only would the weight of his body pull against the nails in his hands and feet but that the weight of all the sin in the world would also be laid upon him. He cried out for another way, another choice. But then in one powerful word—*nevertheless*—he surrendered all to the will of his Father.

Therefore, I urge you, brothers and sisters, in view of God's mercy, to offer your bodies as a living sacrifice, holy and pleasing to God—this is your true and proper worship. Do not conform to the pattern of this world, but be transformed by the renewing of your mind. Then you will be able to test and approve what God's will is—his good, pleasing and perfect will.

Romans 12:1–2

Sacrifice. *Living* sacrifice. Serving others, loving others, preferring others, living for God's purposes and not our own—this is sacrificial living. This is crucifying our flesh, our self-focused ways, and choosing instead the ways of God: love, joy, peace, patience, kindness, goodness, faithfulness, gentleness, and self-control. We can live in such a way only if we die to ourselves and live instead for him—continuously, no longer conformed to this world but transformed according to his will.

And here is the mystery and beauty of it all: The more we pour ourselves out in living sacrifice, the more God's love pours into us—oceans of it, overflowing, spilling out onto every life we touch, every baton we carry, every handoff we release. We are filled and refilled with the ceaseless, unstoppable love of God. AND WE RUN!

We run to a world that does not know him but desperately needs him. We run to neighbors in distress, to girls locked in brothels, to children in hunger, to friends in pain. We run to the next generation and welcome them to the race. We run, fueled by the passion of the fullness of God's love pouring into us and through us to a broken, dying world "so loved" by God that he sent his only Son, who drank the Winner's Cup of sacrificial love.

> *"My command is this: Love each other as I have loved you. Greater love has no one than this: to lay down one's life for one's friends. You are my friends if you do what I command. I no longer call you servants, because a servant does not know his master's business. Instead, I have called you friends, for everything that I learned from my Father I have made known to you."*
> John 15:12–15

In the book of Romans, Paul tells us how urgent it is that we be about our Father's business.

> *Make sure that you don't get so absorbed and exhausted in taking care of all your day-by-day obligations that you lose track of the time and doze off, oblivious to God. The night is about over, dawn is about to break. Be up and awake to what God is doing! God is putting the finishing touches on the salvation work he began when we first believed. We can't afford to waste a minute, must not squander these precious daylight*

hours in frivolity and indulgence, in sleeping around and dissipation, in bickering and grabbing everything in sight. Get out of bed and get dressed! Don't loiter and linger, waiting until the very last minute. Dress yourselves in Christ, and be up and about!

Romans 13:11–14 MSG

This earth is not our home. Knowing this helps us to hold more loosely to the comforts of this earth and to reach ever forward to grasp the things of God, willing to say our own "Nevertheless, not my will but yours be done."

Kalli says "nevertheless" when she closes her eyes at night and must wrestle with the images of the horrific ordeals she's heard from the girls in the safe house.

Kristen says "nevertheless" as she speaks to educators about lifesaving curriculum while sacrificing her nights and weekends to study for her university degree.

Favour's "nevertheless" is sharing her new Christian faith while continuing to do the hard work of healing and forgiving.

Annie's "nevertheless" is her continued sacrifice in Greece, across the ocean from her family, whom she still misses painfully.

Phil continues living out his "nevertheless" in his

willingness to never stop praying, *Lord, break my heart for what breaks yours.* He forever carries with him the image of the little girl in Cambodia whose teeth were brutally kicked in as she was raped. Nevertheless, Phil gladly keeps seeking out victims to help. He is spurred on by the Lord he loves, who *"for the joy set before him . . . endured the cross, scorning its shame, and sat down at the right hand of the throne of God"* (Hebrews 12:2).

Nick and I had a new "nevertheless" experience during the writing of this book. We had known for the past year that Nick's mother's health was declining. This great woman had birthed fifteen children and had a special gift to hold the family together.

Then, a few months ago, while I was speaking at an event in Kansas City, one of Nick's sisters called with the news that his mother had fallen and was rushed to the hospital. In a coma, she was not expected to make it through that day.

Even if Nick had jumped on a plane that very second, there was no way he could possibly get home to Australia in time.

His sister put the phone to his mother's ear, and Nick spoke his final words to his mother across the world while she was in a coma. Nick knew he would never see his mother again. Within a few hours, she was gone, and Nick, through his grief, made plans for the long trip home to take part in her funeral.

When we said yes to starting A21 and moving away from Australia, we both left behind aging mothers, all our family, and lifelong friends. Would we have loved to be there with Nick's mother in those final hours? Yes. But nevertheless. Had we responsibly made provision for our mothers in every way? Yes. Do we both call our families frequently? Yes. Did we ask God to keep Nick's mum alive so he could be there? Yes. Did she still get promoted to heaven before he could get home? Yes. Am I aware that my own mother is not getting any younger? Yes.

Are there moments we consider handing it all over and going back home to the familiar and comfortable? No. Nick and I continue to say, "Nevertheless, Lord! Not my will, but yours, be done." Yes, life is hard and painful sometimes, but Jesus is good. God's grace is sufficient.

What is your nevertheless?

Your spouse may have abandoned you, but nevertheless you will remain a faithful parent committed to raising godly children. You may be tempted to indulge your desires, but nevertheless you will remain morally pure. You may have the opportunity to misuse your access to funds at work, but nevertheless you choose to live a God-honoring life. You may have been deeply wounded by another person, but nevertheless you will forgive. Your boss may be abusing her power and mistreating your team, but nevertheless your response will be above reproach. You may be longing for that next "fix"—be it a substance, a habit, an online site, an illicit relationship, a purchase you cannot afford—but nevertheless you choose obedience and freedom. You lay down yourself and lift up your Lord. You choose to be last and put Christ first. You die to self so that you may live in Christ. Nevertheless!

BORN TO WIN

Our first birth destined us to lose because *we were born into sin*. But because of Jesus's "nevertheless" decision, because he went to the cross to pay the price for our sin, we have been born again.

> *You have been born again, not of perishable seed, but of imperishable, through the living and enduring word of God.*
>
> 1 Peter 1:23

When we are born again, *we are born to WIN!*

As we run in God's divine relay, we are running in assured victory. We are part of Christ's triumphal procession, because Jesus has already won and his Spirit lives in us.

Thanks be to God, who always leads us as captives in Christ's triumphal procession and uses us to spread the aroma of the knowledge of him everywhere.

2 Corinthians 2:14

What an image! As we run, we spread the aroma of God in our every action and interaction, and we will cross the finish line, unstoppable, into the embrace of our eternal Father God.

God has chosen you. Prepared you. Placed you. Now run into your exchange zone, hand outstretched and open, and grasp every baton he brings your way. Discover that not only are you making a difference in the world, but God is making a difference in you. The world will be forever changed because of *you*.

My life and yours have been touched by batons carried from generation to generation before us, and we will carry them to our culture and every culture on this planet. True victory comes with your lifetime commitment to living in the exchange zone, passing on the baton of faith into the life of one, plus one, plus one ...

Therefore, since we are surrounded by such a great cloud of witnesses, let us throw off everything that hinders and the sin that so easily entangles. And

let us run with perseverance the race marked out
for us, fixing our eyes on Jesus, the pioneer and
perfecter of faith.

Hebrews 12:1–2

You know what God has called you to do, so run, unstoppable, until the day you cross the finish line and hear the words of your father, *"Well done, good and faithful servant!...Come and share your master's happiness!"* (Matthew 25:21).

Now may the God of peace, who through the blood
of the eternal covenant brought back from the dead
our Lord Jesus, that great Shepherd of the sheep,
equip you with everything good for doing his will,
and may he work in us what is pleasing to him,
through Jesus Christ, to whom be glory for ever
and ever. Amen.

Hebrews 13:20–21

NOTES

CHAPTER 1

1. https://www.olympic.org/sydney-2000/athletics
   /4x100m-relay-women.
2. http://espn.go.com/olympics/summer/2012
   /trackandfield/story/_/id/8256748/2012-london
   -olympics-us-shatters-women-4–4x100-relay
   -world-record.
3. https://www.olympic.org/london-2012/athletics
   /4x100m-relay-women.

CHAPTER 2

1. Moses's initial protests to God's call are recorded
   in Exodus 3:6–4:14. Gideon's doubts and protests
   are found in Judges 6. Jeremiah's feelings of
   inadequacy and the Lord's response to them are
   found in Jeremiah 1:4–10. Mary, perplexed at how

she, a virgin, could give birth to the Son of God, was humbled and willing, as recorded in Luke 1:26–55.

2. "Human trafficking is the second largest global organized crime today, generating approximately 31.6 billion USD each year. Specifically, trafficking for sexual exploitation generates 27.8 billion USD per year," United Nations Office on Drugs and Crime, 2009, "Trafficking in Persons: Global Patterns," http://www.unodc.org /documents/human-trafficking/Global_Report _on_TIP.pdf.

3. "800,000—Number of people trafficked across international borders every year," US Department of State, "Trafficking in Persons Report: 2007." "Tragically, only 1–2 percent of victims are rescued, and only 1 in 100,000 Europeans involved in trafficking are convicted," from United Nations, "UN Agency Calls for Better Monitoring to Combat Human Trafficking in Europe," in UN News Centre, 2009, https://news.un.org/en /story/2009/10/317642.

CHAPTER 3

1. Mark 6:30–44; Luke 9:10–17; Matthew 14:13–21; John 6:1–15.

CHAPTER 4

1. 1 Samuel 16:1–13.

CHAPTER 6

1. Moses's encounter with Pharaoh's chariots at the Red Sea is found in Exodus 14. Joshua's experience of bringing down the walls of Jericho is recorded in Joshua 6. Gideon's defeat of the Midianite army can be read in Judges 7. Peter's walk on water is told in Matthew 14:22–32.

CHAPTER 8

1. Today, A21 has fourteen offices in twelve countries, with plans for even more growth.
2. Exodus 17:8–13.

CHAPTER 9

1. https://www.lexico.com/en/definition/passion.

CHAPTER 10

1. Matthew 4:1–11.
2. Matthew 26.
3. https://2009-2017.state.gov/j/tip/rls/tiprpt/2012/192362.htm.